Winter on the Farm

Matthew Evans

Photography by Alan Benson

MURDOCH BOOKS

Contents

Introduction

Winter. Just the word has a ring to it; a sense that, even if you're closer to the equator than I am, it's a time of cold weather and mittens, beanies and long overcoats. Winter, by its very nature, seems to suggest steamy breath, frosty mornings and windows fogged up by slow cooking.

Winter is a season to be adored on the farm. A time of hibernation, with less work to do in the garden and more excuses to pull up the pouf, get out the granny rug for the legs and read a book. Trees are stripped bare, letting the low sun shine golden when it appears. On rainy mornings mist as thick as meringue clings to the top of hills surrounding the valley. The ground crackles underfoot after strikingly cold clear nights, when you have to break the ice in the cow's water trough.

The start of winter is signified by the sound of chainsaws and splitters, as the last of the firewood is stacked and dried — a job best started in summer, but always improved if the stack is large. We fire up a Rayburn woodfired cooker in the cooler months, the water jacket at the back heating our showers to scalding. In this cooker tougher meats are rendered to buttery softness overnight, the house filling with smells of lamb with wild fennel, beef in stout, or duck cooked in a little red wine. The aroma of slow-cooked beans or chickpeas with meats wafts up to my bedroom from below and my dreams are laced with grand meals.

Mid-winter and the vegetable garden is full of leafy greens ready for picking — kale, cauliflower and broccoli, along with ox heart cabbages and the last of the carrots and beetroot. Nights are long and drinks warm. The thermometer offers an excuse to stay indoors for cups of tea with biscuits. It is an excuse always at hand and often used.

By the end of winter the asparagus has started to break the earth. Artichokes have begun to ball up ready to flower. Rhubarb, some at least, is on its march and the days are longer, if not exactly warmer. Garlic is in the ground, but not doing much. Broad beans are leafy, but a long way from producing a crop. The ewes are heavy with lamb and the chooks have started laying again. Snow can be seen on the caps of wild peaks in the distance, and the pigs are foraging longer into the evening. The wattle flowers across the valley and daffodils that have pushed their way through the soil in the yard release their cheery smiles. Spring is just around the corner, but there's still time for pork chops with mustard and beer, a white bean and sausage soup, and plenty more steamed marmalade pudding.

Sleep-in food

The nights are long, gloriously long and the days abbreviated by winter. It's easier, I find, to lie in when there's little light and the day outside is yet to shake off its frosty cover. This is the time for cooked food, for hot honeyed polenta with stewed apple or eggy French toast stuffed with the preserved fruits of autumn. Winter pancakes are laced with salted caramel pears and finished with rum. The corned beef from a couple of nights ago is turned into hash and topped with an egg. Tea is brought steaming into the bedroom and the coffee machine works overtime. Whatever else there is to do, it's time to linger over brunch.

Recipes

The perfect date and banana porridge

(and it doesn't have to take hours to cook)
serves 2

Good hot porridge is better than a duck-down doona. Better than a hug from Mum or a hot bath and warm slippers. Yet, winter's marvellous breakfast food seems to be filled with mystique. Some think it takes hours to cook. Some aren't sure what the texture should be like (not soupy, but runny enough to pour most of it from the pan). For some reason we don't have the few minutes it takes to cook porridge, which is a shame, as the instant alternative tastes a lot like floor sweepings pretending to be oats. Good oats for porridge are soft. Ideally they're rolled between stones (there are some out there), but most importantly the oats mustn't be hard or firm. The best oats for porridge have a soft, downy look to them when you peer through the bag. Ideally you'd soak the oats in water overnight and cook them for an hour, but you don't have to. Always start with cold water, you can add boiling water later.

Put the oats in a saucepan with at least 250 ml (9 fl oz/1 cup) cold water. Place over high heat and bring to the boil. Reduce the heat to low and simmer, then add about 375 ml (13 fl oz/1½ cups) water (cold or boiling, depending on what kind of hurry you're in). Stir minimally and simmer very gently for about 5 minutes, or until the texture is creamy, but definitely not gluey (if you've pre-soaked the oats, they won't even take that long). Stirring them or using dodgy oats (such as instant porridge) will make it gluey. Tip in a little hot water if it's too thick. Add the salt, dates and banana and cook for 1 minute longer. Stir in a little cream and brown sugar, then serve the porridge hot with more cream and sugar on the table.

Note: Organic bananas aren't gassed, so they ripen slower and taste better. Non-organic bananas can be used, too.

100 g (3½ oz/1 cup) soft rolled (porridge) oats
a generous pinch of salt
4 big fleshy fresh dates, chopped (if using dried dates, add to the oats at the start of cooking)
1 ungassed ripe banana (see note), chopped
pouring (whipping) cream or milk, to serve
soft brown sugar, to taste

Mushrooms on toast

serves 4

Roasted mushrooms are heavenly on toast. Try to buy big mushrooms because they have a lot more flavour, and if you can chargrill your bread it'll taste so much better. If you use small mushrooms be aware that they will cook more quickly.

Preheat the oven to 180°C (350°F/Gas 4).

Toss the mushrooms in a bowl with the bay leaves, thyme, olive oil and garlic. Arrange in a single layer on a baking tray and bake for about 30 minutes, or until the mushrooms have become tender, dark and wonderful.

Serve the mushrooms hot on chargrilled bread, or keep them for an antipasto platter.

1 kg (2 lb 4 oz) field mushrooms or Swiss brown mushrooms
2 bay leaves
2 thyme sprigs, torn into pieces
a goodly amount of extra virgin olive oil
3 garlic cloves
8 generous slices sourdough bread, chargrilled or toasted, to serve

Breakfast semolina

serves 2–3

Yes, you may have grown up eating it. And yes, it does still taste just as good, like nursery food should. Semolina is comfort food at its most basic — a warm, milky gruel with a moussey texture that just has to have jam stirred in to make it exciting. Joanna's Jam is the best bought version I've found in Tasmania. You can finish this dish with two drops of rosewater and serve with a sprinkling of chopped pistachios if you want to be fancy.

Put the milk, semolina and salt in a saucepan and bring to the boil, stirring constantly so it doesn't form lumps. Reduce the heat to low and simmer, stirring occasionally, for about 10 minutes, or until the consistency is nice and thick.

   Serve the semolina in bowls with the raspberry jam on the table. Add a spoonful of jam to each bowl of semolina and nibble a little of this with each mouthful.

1 litre (35 fl oz/4 cups) milk
130 g (4¾ oz/⅔ cup) coarse
   breakfast semolina
a generous pinch of salt
raspberry jam, to serve

Tell me a joke and sing me a song, stroke my brow gently and cuddle me along. It's the weekend today, with comforting food, so let's have a slow brekky to get me into the mood.

Corned beef hash

serves 4

The trick to making good hash browns is getting the potato to stick together. I reckon this is best done by par-cooking them to change the starch's character — but beware, as cooking times will vary enormously depending on varieties and the age of the potatoes you use. This recipe makes a modest amount, so I suggest making a big batch to use over coming days. Plan on making it after having corned beef for dinner if you want to avoid double work.

Steam or boil the potatoes whole until they're nearly cooked, but retain some firmness. Rinse in cold water until they are cool enough to handle, then use a knife to rub off the skin (this works best while the potatoes are still warm). Mash or coarsely grate the potatoes.

Mix the warm mashed potato with the corned beef and season with salt (remembering the corned beef is salty) and freshly ground black pepper.

Melt a little butter in a frying pan over medium heat. Add the leek and cook for 5 minutes, or until softened. Add to the potato and corned beef mixture and allow to cool.

Divide the potato mixture into eight portions and use your hands to roll each portion into a ball — you may need to mash it all up and press it together to get it to stick.

Heat a little more butter in a large, heavy-based frying pan over medium heat. Gently squash the potato balls into the pan to make patties and cook for about 3–5 minutes, or until deep brown on one side, then turn and cook the other side, adding just a touch more butter if you like.

Serve the corned beef hash with soft poached eggs and perhaps some roasted mushrooms (see page 14) and sambal oelek on the side.

400 g (14 oz/about 2) white-fleshed potatoes such as desiree or king edward, washed, unpeeled

200 g (7 oz) corned beef (see page 136), shredded with your hands

butter, for frying

¼ leek, white part only, finely chopped (or use onion)

4 poached free-range eggs, to serve

sambal oelek or tomato sauce (ketchup), to serve

Honeyed breakfast polenta

serves 2–3

This is a wonderfully light gruel that goes really well with berry jam if you run out of honey. Just replace the honey with the same amount of sugar, and use jam on top. You can also use a compote of dried fruit instead of the jam.

Put the milk and 500 ml (17 fl oz/2 cups) water in a saucepan over high heat. As it comes to a simmer, sprinkle in the polenta, stirring the whole time — you don't want it to form clumps. Bring back to the boil, stirring continuously, then reduce the heat to low and simmer for 10 minutes, stirring occasionally until the polenta has a nice porridge consistency (if it spits, and it well may, a lid helps cut down on the cleaning).

Add the butter, honey and salt and stir well to combine. Serve the polenta with extra honey passed separately so people can sweeten the polenta to their liking. It also tastes great with hot stewed fruits dolloped on top.

500 ml (17 fl oz/2 cups) milk
190 g (6¾ oz/1 cup) polenta
a good knob (25 g/1 oz or whatever your cardiologist will allow) of butter
1 tablespoon good-quality honey, plus extra, to serve
a generous pinch of salt

Thank goodness for honey. For the bees that fertilise the garden, the flowers and the wattle that lines the creek bed. I eat so much of the nectar, scented by the blossoms of prickly box or leatherwood or stringy bark, that I sometimes feel like Winnie the Pooh. With a penchant for cake.

Yoghurt pancakes with drunken brown sugar salted pears

makes 12 pancakes

I know a sweet young boy whose favourite joke is 'What's brown and sticky?' The answer, of course, is a stick. But I actually can't help thinking of brown sugar and pears when I think of brown and sticky. And who can go past pancakes stacked up underneath? Certainly not the little boy inside me. I like to use two pans to cook pancakes so it speeds up the process. Put the oven on to warm the plates and to keep the pancakes hot as you go. If you don't have any plain yoghurt, use 1 tablespoon of lemon juice with an extra 2 tablespoons of milk.

To make the drunken pears, heat 20 g (¾ oz) of the butter in a saucepan or frying pan over medium heat and gently cook the pears for 5–8 minutes, or until softened. Add the brown sugar and half of the salt and stir to dissolve. Remove from the heat and add the rum. Set aside.

To make the pancakes, beat together the eggs, caster sugar and remaining salt, then whisk in the milk and yoghurt. Add enough flour to get a thick consistency that will still pour from a ladle — you can always add more milk or flour as you go. Melt the remaining butter and stir through.

Heat a little extra butter in a frying pan over medium–low heat and ladle in 2 tablespoons of the pancake batter to make a circle with a 10 cm (4 inch) diameter. Cook until it is brown on the underside and bubbles appear on the top, then turn it over to brown on the other side. Remove to a plate and keep warm in the oven. Repeat with the remaining batter to make 12 pancakes in total.

Serve the pancakes in stacks with the pear spooned over (including any juices) and the cream on the table.

50 g (1¾ oz) butter, plus extra, for cooking
2 large ripe pears, peeled, quartered, cored and cut into thick slices
3 tablespoons soft brown sugar
½ teaspoon salt
1 tablespoon brown rum
2 eggs
1 tablespoon caster (superfine) sugar
250 ml (9 fl oz/1 cup) milk
3 tablespoons plain yoghurt
135 g (4¾ oz) self-raising flour
pouring (whipping) cream, to serve

Here's the deal. You make me a cuppa to have in bed,
    and I'll cook brunch — something to celebrate winter.
Something satisfying, rich and very sweet. Oh all right
    then, if you ask me nicely and let me lie in for another
ten minutes, I'll do both.

Cardamom-scented rice pudding with baked rhubarb

serves 4–6

In some places rhubarb grows throughout the year, making it the perfect foil for a hot milky pudding. I've suggested having this for breakfast, mainly because I often bake it in the cooling woodfired cooker overnight, but it's just as good after dinner, or instead of dinner on a day when you don't really mind.

Preheat the oven to 220°C (425°F/Gas 7). To make the baked rhubarb, arrange the rhubarb in a single layer in a baking tray and sprinkle over the sugar. Bake for about 10–15 minutes, or until tender. Set aside until ready to serve. Baked rhubarb will keep stored in an airtight container in the refrigerator for up to 7 days.

Reduce the oven temperature to 140°C (275°F/Gas 1).

To make the rice pudding, place the milk, cream, lemon zest, cardamom and vanilla bean and seeds in a large saucepan and bring to a simmer. Turn off the heat and leave to stand for 15 minutes to allow the flavours to infuse. Discard the vanilla bean and pour the mixture into a 20 cm (8 inch) round casserole dish. Add the sugar and stir until it dissolves, then stir in the rice until well combined.

Bake the pudding for 1½ hours, or until cooked, stirring occasionally if you feel like it. I don't because I like the 'fly's walk' or the skin that forms on the top of rice pudding. I tend to find the pudding may be a little runny after 1½ hours, with the rice grains plump yet still retaining their integrity, but it will thicken up more as it cools.

Serve the pudding warm with the baked rhubarb, and keep the serving dish for the cook to scrape. You do have to avoid the cardamom pods, but I kind of like that buzz when you nibble on one.

BAKED RHUBARB
1 small bunch rhubarb, trimmed and cut into 3 cm (1¼ inch) pieces
70 g (2½ oz/⅓ cup) soft brown sugar

RICE PUDDING
625 ml (21½ fl oz/2½ cups) milk
125 ml (4 fl oz/½ cup) pouring (whipping) cream
finely grated zest of 1 lemon
5 large cardamom pods
1 vanilla bean, split lengthways
90 g (3¼ oz) raw (demerara) sugar
80 g (2¾ oz/⅓ cup) short-grain white rice

French toast stuffed with poached pear

serves 4

To stuff French toast, you make a pocket in the bread to fill. It's easier to handle than making a sandwich, though that works well, too. If you don't have poached pears, soften slices of peeled and cored pears in a little butter in the frying pan before cooking the toast, adding a pinch of salt for real excitement.

Cut a slit into one side of each slice of bread to make a large flat pocket. Slip in about half a pear's worth of fruit. Combine the egg, milk, vanilla and maple syrup in a large, flat bowl.

Heat a large frying pan over medium heat and add a generous knob of butter. Working with one piece of bread at a time, dip it into the egg mixture until well sodden, then transfer straight to the pan where the butter should have just started to sizzle. Cook to brown one side, then turn and cook the other — you may want to use a lid to warm it right through and you'll probably need to cook the toast in two batches.

Serve the toast drizzled with extra maple syrup and some cream on the side if you like. Make sure there's plenty of syrup on the table for those greedy enough to want more. Or even better, if you've poached your own fruit use the poaching syrup in its place.

4 slices bread cut from an unsliced white loaf, about 3–4 cm (1¼–1½ inches) thick
2 pears, poached and sliced
5 eggs, lightly beaten with a generous pinch of salt
80 ml (2½ fl oz/⅓ cup) milk
¼ teaspoon vanilla paste or 1 teaspoon natural vanilla extract
2 tablespoons maple syrup, plus extra, to serve
butter, for cooking
lightly whipped cream, to serve (optional)

Substantial soups

Forget your thin little broths of summer, your lightly cooked potages that bring relief from proper meals on hot days. In winter you want soup that sticks, soup that becomes the meal.

Winter means dried beans surrendering themselves into simmering broth. Root vegetables and meat. Bacon-flavoured stock used with abandon, or a pea and ham soup enlivened with meyer lemon. Sausages are sliced, parsnips are diced and onions fried. A huge vat of soup can fuel you through many meals, especially when leftovers are spirited away to the freezer for those days when you want the joy of a slow-cooked soup, but can't commit the time.

Recipes

Beer, cheese and onion soup

serves 6

This dark onion soup is a good dish for those days when you don't have any beef stock; you can use water instead. Beer, while not essential, adds a savoury character to the sweet nature of the onions. The frying of the onions to get that dark golden but unburnt colour means it's best if you've got quite a bit of time to spend hanging around the stove.

Heat the butter in a large saucepan over low heat and cook the onion slowly, stirring often, until the onion is soft and turns a lovely golden brown — this could take a while, so allow at least 30 minutes. I like to add salt as the onion cooks to even up the cooking and help draw out moisture. As it cooks, add the thyme and bay leaf. Pour in the beer and stock, add the parsley and pepper and simmer for 1 hour.

To serve, top the baguette slices with the cheese and toast under a preheated grill (broiler) until golden. Ladle the soup into bowls and float two slices of bread on top, or serve it on the side.

60 g (2¼ oz) butter or lard, or 3 tablespoons oil
8 large onions, very thinly sliced
a generous pinch of salt
3 thyme sprigs
1 bay leaf
100 ml (3½ fl oz) dark beer (but not quite stout)
875 ml (30 fl oz/3½ cups) beef stock or water
1 cup chopped flat-leaf (Italian) parsley
½ teaspoon freshly ground black pepper
1 small baguette, cut on an angle into 12 thick slices
200 g (7 oz/2 cups) grated gruyére cheese or other good melting cheese

Cawl (Welsh leek soup)

serves 8–10

This soup, pronounced more like 'cowl', traditionally uses meat stock; its variation is only limited by whatever meats or vegetables are on hand. You could use leftover pork broth from the twice-cooked shoulder (see page 140) or some of the juices from the Sicilian-style braised lamb shoulder (see page 132). Alternatively, you could throw a bit of lamb in a pot with some water to make a broth, or just use water and let the brisket do the trick.

Heat the lard in a large heavy-based saucepan that has a tight-fitting lid (cast-iron is perfect) over medium heat. Cook the bay leaves, carrot, celery and three-quarters of the leek for 8–10 minutes, or until tender but not brown. Pour in the stock, bring to the boil, then add the thyme and beef brisket.

Cover the pan, reduce the heat to low, and simmer for about 1½ hours, then add the parsnip, potato and cabbage and simmer for at least another 30 minutes, or until the vegetables are surrendering themselves to the broth and melting apart. Add the remaining leek and simmer for a further 5 minutes, or until just cooked.

To serve, you can strip the meat from the beef brisket and add back to the soup. Like a lot of soups, this one is excellent served the next day.

20 g (¾ oz) lard, bacon fat or butter

2 fresh bay leaves

2 large carrots, chopped

4 celery stalks, chopped

4 large leeks, white part only, rinsed and thinly sliced

3.5 litres (120 fl oz) meat stock, broth or water

3 thyme sprigs or a pinch of dried thyme

250 g (9 oz) chunk beef brisket

2 parsnips, chopped

4 all-purpose potatoes, such as pontiac, diced

350 g (12 oz/about ¼ small) cabbage, roughly chopped

It was a frosty morning, hand-milking the cow. And the chooks seemed ravenous when I let them out of their coop. I've spent an hour watching the graceful lines of Indian runner ducks trotting along just beyond the front porch and there's a peaceful lowing on the breeze. Even if you've just fought the crowds at the shops and there are sirens in the air, at least soup makes it feel like you're back on the farm.

Sausage and white bean soup

serves 6

Keep your old parmesan rind and ham skin to add extra flavour to soups like this, then simply discard them before serving.

Heat the olive oil in a large saucepan or stockpot over medium heat and cook the sausages for 5–10 minutes, turning as needed, until well browned. Remove from the pan, cut into bite-sized pieces and set aside.

Add the onion to the pan and cook for 5 minutes, or until softened, then add the carrot and celery and cook for 5 minutes, without colouring. Return the sausage pieces to the pan, add the white beans, parmesan rind, ham skin and stock. Bring to the boil, then reduce the heat to low and simmer for 1½ hours, or until the beans are very tender. Season with salt and freshly ground black pepper (remembering the snags, rind and skin will already be adding some flavour) and serve with a drizzle of extra virgin olive oil, and crusty bread if you like.

1 tablespoon olive oil

300 g (10½ oz) pure pork sausages

2 large onions, diced

2 carrots, diced

3 celery stalks, diced

300 g (10½ oz) dried white (northern) beans, soaked overnight, rinsed and drained

50 g (1¾ oz) parmesan cheese rind

90 g (3¼ oz) ham or prosciutto skin

1.5 litres (52 fl oz/6 cups) roasted chicken stock (see page 54)

extra virgin olive oil, to serve

Time to lay the table and time to talk.
Time for lingering over slow-simmered soups. It's winter,
so there should be more time for the things that matter.
And a lot of things that don't.

Michelle's sweet spiced oxtail and parsnip soup

serves 6–8

My friend, Michelle, who helped test recipes for this book, took my idea for a very European-style soup and did this to it. With its spice and deep golden hue, it's heavenly. She recommends adding a big handful of finely chopped kale to finish it off beautifully.

Preheat the oven to 200°C (400°F/Gas 6). Rub the oxtail pieces with some extra olive oil to coat all over, season with salt and freshly ground black pepper and place in a roasting tin. Roast for 1 hour, or until dark. Drain on paper towels.

Meanwhile, heat the olive oil in a large saucepan or stockpot over medium heat and cook the onion for 10 minutes, or until softened and starting to brown. Add the parsnip and cook for 1–2 minutes, then add the garlic and ginger. Reduce the heat to low, add the turmeric, cumin, cloves and nutmeg and simmer for 3–4 minutes, or until it smells delicious, being carfeul not to scorch the spices. Remove from the heat, add the oxtails and set aside.

Add 500 ml (17 fl oz/2 cups) hot water to the roasting tin with the oxtail cooking juices and cook over medium heat, scraping up any sticky brown bits stuck to the tin, and stirring for 1–2 minutes, or until the sauce is dark brown and bubbling.

Add the sauce to the oxtails in the pan, then add 2 litres (70 fl oz/8 cups) water and the tomato passata, and season to taste with salt and freshly ground black pepper. Bring to the boil, then reduce the heat and simmer for at least 1 hour, or preferably 2 hours. You may need to skim off some of the fat at this stage. Pick the meat off the bones and stir back into the soup before serving.

600 g (1 lb 5 oz) oxtail, cut into rounds

2 tablespoons olive oil, plus extra, for rubbing

2 onions, thinly sliced

4 parsnips, cut into bite-sized chunks

2 garlic cloves, crushed

1 cm (½ inch) piece of ginger, grated

½ teaspoon ground turmeric

1 teaspoon ground cumin

½ teaspoon ground cloves

½ teaspoon freshly ground nutmeg

125 g (4½ oz/½ cup) tomato passata (puréed tomatoes)

Chunky barley and mushroom soup with bacon broth

serves 6

Bacon bones often don't have any salt added, but sometimes, weirdly, they do, so allow for that when cooking. In their absence you could use a ham hock or similar and strip the meat from the hock to add back into the soup. Or, simply cook 100 g (3½ oz) bacon strips with the onions at the start of cooking.

Heat the olive oil in a large flameproof casserole dish over medium heat. Add the bacon bones and turn to coat in the oil, then cook for about 2–3 minutes. Stir in the onion and break the mushrooms into chunks with your fingers and add those too. Cook for 10–15 minutes, stirring occasionally until it smells delicious and the vegetables start to brown.

Add the carrot, celery, bay leaf, garlic and thyme to the dish and cook for 3–4 minutes, then add the paprika, barley and 2 litres (70 fl oz/8 cups) water and bring to the boil. Reduce the heat and simmer for 1½ hours, or until the barley is soft and creamy. If the soup becomes too thick you may need to add some water, even as much as 1 litre (35 fl oz/4 cups) water, because barley swells and swells, and water evaporates as you cook. It could just as easily take 3 hours to cook, which isn't a bad thing at all with soup. Remove the bacon bones and stir through the parsley to serve.

1–2 tablespoons olive oil, plus 2 tablespoons extra
500 g (1 lb 2 oz) bacon bones
2 onions, diced
350 g (12 oz) field or Swiss brown mushrooms
2 carrots, diced
1 celery stalk, diced
1 bay leaf
2 garlic cloves
3–4 thyme sprigs
½ teaspoon sweet smoked paprika
200 g (7 oz/1 cup) barley, rinsed and drained
1 cup chopped flat-leaf (Italian) parsley

Lamb and tomato soup with yoghurt

serves 4

I like the idea of thickening this soup slightly with a yoghurt custard. I know tomatoes aren't a winter vegetable, but the tinned ones can be wonderful and sometimes you need an additional flavour in the cooler months. In order to make the lamb broth you will need to roast the lamb necks first by lightly oiling them and then cooking on a baking tray in a 220°C (425°F/Gas 7) oven for 40–60 minutes, or until well browned all over, turning as necessary.

To make the lamb broth, place the lamb necks in a large saucepan or stockpot with the leek, carrot, celery and parsley stalks. Add 4–5 litres (140–175 fl oz) water and bring to the boil. Remove any impurities by skimming the surface as it comes to a simmer, then reduce the heat to low, add the bay leaves, thyme and peppercorns and simmer for about 2 hours. Strain and discard the vegetables and herbs — you should have about 3 litres (105 fl oz) of stock. If you want, you can pick the meat from the bone. (You should. You really should.) Lamb broth can be stored in an airtight container in the refrigerator for up to 3 days or in the freezer for up to 3 months.

To make the lamb and tomato soup with yoghurt, heat the olive oil in a large saucepan or stockpot over high heat and cook the onion for about 1–2 minutes, or until starting to colour. Add the carrot, celery and parsley, and continue to cook for 5–6 minutes, or until softened but not browned. Add the tomato and lamb broth (including the lamb meat, if you want), and simmer for about 1 hour; season with salt and freshly ground black pepper.

In a small bowl, whisk together the yoghurt, egg and paprika, then add to the soup and continue to whisk until combined. Turn off the heat and let the yoghurt custard set in the soup. Serve hot.

LAMB BROTH

- 2 lamb necks, roasted (see introduction)
- 2 leeks, white part only, rinsed and chopped
- 2 carrots, chopped
- 2 celery stalks, chopped
- 4 flat-leaf (Italian) parsley stalks
- 3 bay leaves
- 1 thyme sprig
- 1 tablespoon black peppercorns

- 1–2 tablespoons olive oil
- 1 large red onion, finely chopped
- 1 carrot, finely chopped
- 1 celery stalk, finely chopped
- ½ bunch flat-leaf (Italian) parsley, chopped
- 400 g (14 oz) tinned chopped tomatoes
- 300 g (10½ oz) plain yoghurt
- 2 eggs, lightly beaten
- 1 teaspoon sweet paprika

Garlic, potato and paprika soup

serves 4

I prefer to use roasted chicken stock for most recipes, including this one. You can use a chicken frame left over from a good roast dinner, ideally, or buy some bones and roast them until golden in a 220°C (425°F/Gas 7) oven for 40 minutes.

To make the roasted chicken stock, put all of the ingredients in a large saucepan or stockpot over high heat. Add 2 litres (70 fl oz/8 cups) water and bring to the boil, skimming the surface of impurities as it starts to bubble. Reduce the heat to low and simmer for 2 hours. Strain the stock, discarding the solids; you should have about 1.5 litres (52 fl oz/6 cups) of stock, though this varies on the pan and the rate it simmers. The stock can be stored in an airtight container in the refrigerator for up to 5 days or frozen for up to 3 months.

To make the garlic, potato and paprika soup, heat the olive oil in a large saucepan over medium heat and gently cook the onion for 5 minutes, or until softened but not browned. Add the garlic and cook for 3–4 minutes, then stir in the paprika and cook for 30 seconds without scorching. Add half of the diced potato and 800 ml (28 fl oz) of the roasted chicken stock, then season with salt and simmer for 15–20 minutes, or until the potato has softened.

Remove the pan from the heat, allow to cool slightly, then transfer to a blender or use a stick blender to purée until smooth. The soup should have a thinnish character, so add a touch of water if necessary.

Return the soup to a large clean saucepan, add the remaining diced potato and simmer for about 10 minutes, or until tender. Taste again for salt (the potato will have taken some of the seasoning) and serve immediately, possibly with a dollop of sour cream on top.

ROASTED CHICKEN STOCK
1 roasted chicken frame
1 onion, peeled, or use leek or green spring onion (scallion) trimmings
1 carrot, scrubbed
1 celery stalk
1 bay leaf
1 thyme sprig
2 teaspoons white wine vinegar

1 tablespoon olive oil
1 onion, roughly chopped
2 garlic bulbs, cloves peeled
1 teaspoon sweet paprika
800 g (1 lb 12 oz) all-purpose potatoes, peeled and diced
sour cream, to serve (optional)

Winter potato and bacon soup

serves 6–8

A bit thick, a bit chunky and full of smoky bacon flavour, this is the soup you want on a cool day. The quantity of potatoes to broth varies depending on how starchy the spuds are and how thick you want your soup. It will need to cook for at least 3 hours before you can eat it.

Put the bacon bones, onion, carrot, celery, bay leaves and 3 litres (105 fl oz) water in a large saucepan or stockpot over high heat. Bring to the boil, skimming the surface just as it starts to bubble, then reduce the heat, add the peppercorns and thyme and simmer for 2 hours, checking that there's enough water to keep the ingredients covered. Strain the stock, discarding the vegetables — there should be a little over 2 litres (70 fl oz/ 8 cups) stock. Strip any meat from the bones (don't worry if there isn't any), cut into bite-sized pieces and set aside.

Heat the butter in a large clean saucepan over medium heat and cook the leek for 10 minutes, or until soft (a lid helps speed this process). Add the stock and the potato, bring to the boil, then reduce the heat to low and simmer for about 20 minutes, or until the potato is soft, adding more water if necessary.

Remove the pan from the heat, allow to cool slightly, then transfer to a blender or use a stick blender to purée until the soup still has some chunks left in it. Add the bacon meat (and add more fried bacon strips if you like), taste for seasoning and serve immediately.

1 kg (2 lb 4 oz) bacon bones or ham hock, or a mix of both

2 onions, halved

2 carrots, roughly chopped

2–3 celery stalks, roughly chopped

2 bay leaves

1 tablespoon black peppercorns

2 thyme sprigs

a small knob of butter, for frying

2 leeks, white part only, rinsed and shredded

2 kg (4 lb 8 oz) potatoes, peeled, cut into 1 cm (½ inch) dice

Pea, ham and lemon soup

serves 8

The idea for this soup occurred to me when I was eating dal and thought how brilliant it would be to have pea and ham soup enlivened with lemon to try and make it lighter and brighter, while still being as heart-warming as an open fire. So I did it, and it ended up being the food equivalent of having a sauna with a refreshing dip at the end. You don't have to make a ham stock; you can throw the hock, bay leaves, thyme and 4 litres (140 fl oz) water in with the recipe below then fish the hock and herbs out at the end. Making it first however, improves the soup.

To make the ham stock, put all of the ingredients into a large saucepan or stockpot with 4 litres (140 fl oz) water and bring to the boil. Reduce the heat to low and simmer for 2 hours, or until the meat pulls away easily from the bone. Strain the stock, reserving the hock and discarding the herbs and vegetables. Shred the meat from the hock using your fingers and set aside.

To make the pea, ham and lemon soup, heat the butter in a large saucepan or stockpot over medium heat and cook the onion, carrot and celery for about 10 minutes, or until just starting to colour. Add the parsley and cook for 1 minute, then add the peas and ham stock and simmer, stirring occasionally, for about 1½ hours, or until the peas have fallen apart and the soup has thickened slightly — you may need to add more water if it is too thick. Add the meat from the hock and the lemon slices and simmer for a further 5 minutes. Season with salt and freshly ground black pepper (the ham hock adds its own salt that's why it's best to wait until the end), then remove the lemon slices and serve the soup hot on a cold day with crusty bread, if desired.

HAM STOCK
1 kg (2 lb 4 oz) ham hock
2 bay leaves
2 thyme sprigs
2 onions, chopped
2 carrots, chopped

40 g (1½ oz) butter or
  2 tablespoons olive oil
2 large onions, diced
1 carrot, diced
2 celery stalks, diced
¼ cup chopped flat-leaf
  (Italian) parsley
500 g (1 lb 2 oz/2¼ cups)
  green split peas
1 lemon, sliced

Sturdy dishes

Starch — spuds and rice, polenta and pasta — food that isn't hard to digest but doesn't disappear in a minute. Food that fills that hollow feeling inside and lets you know you've eaten. Think, pasta e fagioli and pasta e ceci, dishes that could easily be classified as winter minestrone. Stoups — that strange hybrid of stew and a soup are the order of the day, as are one-pot meals that aren't light on flavour and yet don't challenge the cook. This is my idea of a sturdy meal — one that can fuel you through an afternoon of farm chores without giving you indigestion or leaving you feeling like you'll never be able to eat again.

Recipes

Mussels with white wine and chorizo

serves 4 as a light meal

In Europe they consider the mussel to be best during the cooler months. I'm happy just eating them any time, but with chorizo, they're a standout winter meal. Discard any that don't close when handled before cooking.

Heat the olive oil in a large saucepan or frying pan with a tight-fitting lid over medium heat. Add the garlic and let it sizzle for about 1 minute, stirring often — don't let it brown. Add the chorizo and cook until the fat melts out, again taking care that the garlic doesn't brown. Add the tomato just before it does.

Increase the heat to high, add the wine, bring to the boil, then add the mussels and shake the pan to distribute the heat. Put on the lid and let the mussels steam, shaking the pan every 30 seconds or so to get the mussels mixed up in the juices. After about 5 minutes, possibly less, the mussels will start to open. Continue shaking the pan and checking every minute or so until most, if not all, the mussels are open. Farmed mussels may not all open, but try prising them apart because they're going to be fine if they're fresh.

Serve the mussels and chorizo hot with crusty bread and a good glass of wine on the table.

2 tablespoons extra virgin olive oil
10 garlic cloves, sliced
1 small dried chorizo, skinned and cut into bite-sized pieces
200 g (7 oz) tinned chopped tomatoes
250 ml (9 fl oz/1 cup) dry white wine
2 kg (4 lb 8 oz) mussels, scrubbed and debearded

The snorkel is stashed. The wetsuit is in hibernation. There's no good reason to get in the water, until someone talks about mussels, then it's to buggery with common sense and into the water we go, regardless of the temperature. In some places, however, I presume you can find mussels in the shops.

Pumpkin and meatball risotto

serves 4

I use good-quality sausages and squeeze out the filling to make bite-sized meatballs in this warming northern Italian dish. You could just slice the sausages to cut out a bit of the work, too.

Roll the sausage meat into meatballs with a diameter of about 1.5 cm (⅝ inch). Heat the butter in a large, heavy-based saucepan over medium heat and cook the meatballs, turning them to brown all over. Reduce the heat to low, add the leek and cook for about 4–5 minutes, or until softened. Stir in the pumpkin and rice and continue cooking, stirring regularly, for about 2 minutes.

Add the wine to the pan, increase the heat and continue to stir until all of the wine has been absorbed. Start adding the stock, one ladleful at a time, stirring with a gentle figure eight motion as it cooks to make sure that the rice cooks evenly and that the grains rub together to release some of that creamy starch that makes risotto so wonderful. Season to taste with salt and freshly ground black pepper.

When the stock has been absorbed, stir in another ladleful, and continue to add the stock until it is all used — the time will depend on the type of rice, the heat and your stirring, but check after about 15 minutes — the rice should be firm, but not starchy. Add half of the cheese, stir to combine, then turn off the heat and let the risotto rest for 5 minutes before serving. Serve with the remaining cheese on the table.

200 g (7 oz) pork sausage meat

40 g (1½ oz) butter

200 g (7 oz/about 1 large) leek, white part only, rinsed and finely chopped

200 g (7 oz) pumpkin (squash), grated or cut into 2 mm (¹⁄₁₆ inch) dice

400 g (14 oz/2 cups) risotto rice, such as arborio, vialone nano or carnaroli

200 ml (7 fl oz) good-quality white wine

1.5–2 litres (52–70 fl oz/ 6–8 cups) roasted chicken stock (see page 54), simmering

80 g (2¾ oz) finely grated firm cheese, such as piave, Comté or Italian parmesan cheese

Semolina gnocchi

serves 4

These rich rounds of semolina are usually baked or fried. This is a very rich version that goes really well with just a little butter or sauce.

Put the milk, bay leaf, garlic and a pinch of salt in a large saucepan and bring to the boil. Reduce the heat to low, remove the bay leaf and whisk in the semolina, stirring constantly until it simmers again and there are no lumps. Continue to cook for about 15 minutes, or until thickened, stirring now and then.

   Remove the pan from the heat and stir in the egg yolks, parmesan and nutmeg, then season with salt and freshly ground black pepper. Use a little of the melted butter to grease a 15 x 20 cm (6 x 8 inch) baking tin and spread the gnocchi mixture out evenly so it is about 1 cm (½ inch) thick. Brush with half of the remaining butter then refrigerate for about 2–3 hours. Up to this stage the gnocchi can be prepared a couple of days in advance.

   When ready to serve, cut out circles, each with a 5 cm (2 inch) diameter. Dip each circle first in the extra semolina, flour or cornflour to lightly coat on both sides. Heat the remaining butter in a large frying pan over medium heat and cook the gnocchi for 3–4 minutes on one side, then turn over and cook until the other side is brown. Toss the sage leaves into the pan when you turn the gnocchi and serve. You can serve the gnocchi with a little bit of meat ragu or home-made tomato sauce, if desired.

750 ml (26 fl oz/3 cups) milk
1 bay leaf
1 garlic clove, crushed
a pinch of salt
175 g (6 oz/1 cup) fine semolina
3 egg yolks
80 g (2¾ oz) finely grated Italian parmesan cheese
a generous pinch of freshly grated nutmeg
50 g (1¾ oz) unsalted butter, melted
fine semolina, extra, or plain (all-purpose) flour or cornflour (cornstarch), for dusting
¼ cup sage leaves

Pasta e fagioli

serves 6–8

With an Italian name meaning, quite literally, pasta and beans, this is a 'stoup' — a fabulous cross between a stew and a soup. I've used prosciutto trimmings (the bit the deli can't slice and should sell cheap) though a piece of pancetta or even a very small ham bone would also make a nice broth. If you want a vegetarian version, use parmesan rind instead (but don't fry it) and remove before serving.

Put the white beans in a large saucepan, cover with water and bring to the boil. Add the halved onion and sage sprigs, if using, and simmer for 30 minutes. Drain the beans, discarding the onion and sage, and set aside.

Meanwhile, prepare the vegetables. Heat the olive oil in a large saucepan over low heat and cook the chopped onion for 10 minutes, or until soft. Add the garlic, parsley, prosciutto trimmings, carrot and celery and cook for 5–8 minutes, or until soft. Add 3 litres (105 fl oz) water and bring to the boil. Reduce the heat to low and simmer for about 45 minutes, then add the white beans and continue cooking until the beans are tender — the time will vary between 30 and 60 minutes.

Remove the pan from the heat and discard the prosciutto if it's in a large chunk. Using a ladle, scoop out about one-quarter of the beans and vegetables from the bottom of the pan. Transfer to a blender or food processor and blend or process to a smooth purée. Set aside.

Bring the soup back to the boil and ensure there's enough liquid to cook the pasta. Season with salt and freshly ground black pepper, to taste, then stir in the pasta and simmer for about 10 minutes, or until *al dente*. Return the bean purée to the pan and stir well. Check the consistency (it should be runny, but not thin, though the longer it sits after cooking, the thicker it will get), adding more water if necessary and seasoning, to taste. Serve in big bowls with a little grated parmesan cheese over the top, and an optional drizzle of extra virgin olive oil for added excitement.

400 g (14 oz) dried white (northern) beans, soaked overnight, rinsed and drained
4 large onions, 1 halved and 3 chopped
3–4 sage sprigs (optional)
2 tablespoons olive oil
3 garlic cloves, crushed
2 tablespoons chopped flat-leaf (Italian) parsley
200 g (7 oz) prosciutto trimmings
4 large carrots, diced
6 celery stalks, diced
200 g (7 oz) short pasta, such as ditali
grated Italian parmesan cheese, to serve
extra virgin olive oil (optional), to serve

Cabbage and speck risotto

serves 4–5

My former neighbour, Ros Muirhead, reckoned that when she lived in Milan the sign of a great cook was their cabbage risotto. This is my version. If you use bought stock the end result threatens to be too salty, so better to use more speck and water scented with bay leaf and thyme. Allow 40 minutes for cooking.

Heat the butter in a large saucepan over medium heat and cook the speck to release some of its fat. Add the onion and cook for 5 minutes, stirring occasionally so it doesn't brown. Add the cabbage and salt, cover, and continue to gently cook until the onion has softened. Increase the heat to high, add the rice and cook until it has heated through, then add the wine and stir constantly while the wine evaporates. Reduce the heat to medium and add a ladleful of stock at a time while the rice is still boiling. Risotto loves to be stirred constantly, so the more you do it at the start, the better.

   When the stock has been absorbed, stir in another ladleful and repeat until most of the stock is used, about another 15 minutes — the rice should be firm but not so starchy as to get stuck between your teeth. Different rice varieties take different times, the good stuff takes over 20 minutes, but you don't want to cook it to sludge. When the rice is cooked, add half of the cheese and stir to combine, then turn the heat off and season with salt and freshly ground black pepper. For best results, let the risotto stand for 5 minutes before serving and serve with the remaining cheese on the table, plus a salad or vegetables, if desired.

30 g (1 oz) butter
150 g (5½ oz) speck, pancetta or bacon, finely diced
2 onions, finely diced
½ cabbage, core removed, finely shredded
a generous pinch of salt
400 g (14 oz/2 cups) risotto rice, such as arborio, vialone nano or carnaroli
375 ml (13 fl oz/1½ cups) white wine
2 litres (70 fl oz/8 cups) roasted chicken stock (see page 54), simmering
80 g (2¾ oz) finely grated Italian parmesan cheese

Pasta e ceci

serves 6–8

This is a warming, winter-style chickpea broth with pasta tossed in at the end, similar in some ways to pasta e fagioli (see page 71). You can also flavour it with bacon bones or a bit of prosciutto. For a lesser, but still satisfying result, you can use tinned chickpeas — allow for 3 x 400 g (14 oz) tins (rinsed and drained) and use a lot less water as they won't need much cooking and won't absorb much, if any, water.

Heat the olive oil in a large saucepan or stockpot over low heat and cook the onion for 10 minutes, or until softened. Add the garlic, parsley, carrot and celery and cook for 5–8 minutes, or until soft. Add the stock, parmesan rind, sage and bay leaves and bring to the boil.

Add the chickpeas to the pan and cook for about 1½ hours, or until they are soft. Season to taste with salt and freshly ground black pepper and check that there's enough stock to cook the pasta in. Stir in the pasta and simmer for a further 12 minutes, or until *al dente*, stirring often because the pasta is likely to stick. Remove the parmesan rind and serve with a drizzle of extra virgin olive oil and the grated parmesan on the table.

Variation: You can make a similar dish to this, called *pasta e patate*, by using 800 g (1 lb 12 oz) of potatoes cut into 1 cm (½ inch) dice in place of the chickpeas. Potato takes a lot less cooking, so cook all of the other vegetables for 60 minutes before adding the potato — it should only take about 30 minutes to cook.

2 tablespoons olive oil

3 large onions, cut into 1 cm (½ inch) dice

4 garlic cloves, bruised and chopped

3 tablespoons chopped flat-leaf (Italian) parsley

3 carrots, diced

3 celery stalks, diced

3.5 litres (125 fl oz) vegetable stock

5 cm (2 inch) square piece Italian parmesan cheese rind

1 small sage sprig

2 bay leaves

400 g (14 oz/2 cups) dried chickpeas, soaked overnight, rinsed and drained

200 g (7 oz) short dried pasta, such as shells or ditali

extra virgin olive oil, to serve

grated Italian parmesan cheese, to serve

Buckwheat pasta with potato, Taleggio and sage

serves 4

In Italy's far north they do a dish called pizzoccheri, *baked sometimes, boiled others, but pretty much always a dish of buckwheat pasta with cheese, perhaps Taleggio, cabbage and spuds. You get the slight mealiness of the coarse pasta, the bitterness of cabbage, the starchiness of potato and the sticky stink of good washed rind cheese. I like to cook the spuds and cabbage with the pasta to save on pans and washing up. A flat pasta shape, much closer to pappardelle than lasagne, is ideal.*

Put 5 litres (175 fl oz) water in a large saucepan over high heat and bring to the boil. Add enough salt to give the dish flavour — Italians would use 2 heaped tablespoons, which is a lot. Add the potato and cabbage and simmer for 3 minutes, then add the pasta and stir until it comes back to the boil. Reduce the heat to low and simmer for about 10 minutes, or until the pasta is cooked.

Drain the pasta and vegetables and divide evenly between serving bowls. Dot with the Taleggio cheese and sprinkle over the parmesan. You could put these into a preheated oven at this stage to melt the cheese and keep warm, which wouldn't be a bad thing.

Just before serving, heat the butter in a small frying pan over high heat and add the sage. Shake the pan constantly and when the butter starts to turn nut brown, quickly spoon a little sage and butter over the pasta in each dish and serve immediately.

salt, for cooking

200 g (7 oz) waxy potatoes, such as pink eyes, peeled and cut into 1 cm (½ inch) dice

200 g (7 oz) savoy cabbage, cut into bite-sized pieces

500 g (1 lb 2 oz) buckwheat pasta or other flat, wholemeal pasta

100 g (3½ oz) Taleggio cheese

2 tablespoons grated Italian parmesan cheese

80 g (2¾ oz) butter

20 sage leaves

Finally. Pulled out the hot water bottle and the warm
trousers and the wonderful woolly knits. Thought about
lighting a fire, and then lit both it and the cooker.
Found the bumble bee tea cosy and an excuse to get the
oven going. It's good to know winter's here.

Vodka-cured blue eye potato fish cakes

serves 4

The vodka isn't essential for this, and you could slip it into a glass rather than the curing mixture, but it does add a certain something that is worth trying. You will need to allow at least one day for the fish to marinate.

To make the fennel slaw, toss the fennel, cabbage and mint in a bowl to combine. In a small bowl or in a glass jar with a screw-top lid, put the remaining ingredients and stir or shake to combine. Pour the dressing over the vegetables and toss well to combine. Refrigerate until needed.

To make the fish cakes, pound the garlic, fennel seeds and about 2 teaspoons of the rock salt using a mortar and pestle. Add this to a small bowl with the remaining salt and the vodka and stir to combine. Arrange the fish in a shallow dish, skin side down. Liberally spread the curing mixture all over, then cover with plastic wrap and refrigerate for 24 hours.

Put enough water into a deep frying pan to cover the fish and bring to the boil. Remove the fish from the curing mixture and rinse well. Place in the water and gently poach for 7–10 minutes, or until the fish is just cooked. Remove from the pan and pat dry on paper towels. Cool and flake the fish with your fingers into small pieces, discarding the skin. Set aside.

Preheat the oven to 180°C (350°F/Gas 4). Prick the whole potatoes lightly with a fork and bake for about 1½ hours, or until cooked. Baking keeps the potatoes dry and makes the cakes light and fluffy. When cooked, remove from the oven and either push the flesh through a potato ricer or mouli, or scrape it out of the hard skins with a fork and

FENNEL SLAW

1 large fennel bulb, thinly sliced

200 g (7 oz) cabbage, thinly sliced

1 small bunch mint, finely chopped

1 teaspoon sugar or honey

2 tablespoons freshly squeezed lemon juice

60 ml (2 fl oz/¼ cup) olive oil

½ teaspoon mustard

½ teaspoon salt

continued...

mash into a large mixing bowl. Add the fish, lemon zest, fennel tops, spring onion and some white pepper, and mix well to combine. If the mixture is dry, moisten with a little extra vodka, about 1–2 tablespoons. Divide into eight even portions and use your hands to form eight fish cakes. Refrigerate for 30 minutes.

Set the egg in a bowl on the bench and place the breadcrumbs in a separate bowl. Working with one fish cake at a time, dip it first into the egg and then the breadcrumbs to coat.

Heat a little olive oil in a frying pan over medium–high heat. Add the fish cakes in batches and cook for 4–5 minutes on each side, or until golden brown. Drain on paper towels and serve with the fennel slaw.

FISH CAKES

1 garlic clove
2 tablespoons fennel seeds
100 g (3½ oz/⅓ cup) rock salt
80 ml (2½ fl oz/⅓ cup) vodka
500 g (1 lb 2 oz) blue eye fillets, with skin
800 g (1 lb 12 oz) floury potatoes, such as kennebec or king edward
finely grated zest of 1 large lemon
2 tablespoons chopped green fennel tops
3 spring onions (scallions), finely chopped
2 eggs, lightly beaten
160 g (5¾ oz/2 cups) fresh breadcrumbs
olive oil, for frying

Taragna (buckwheat polenta)

serves 6

Taragna, or buckwheat polenta, which is available from Italian speciality stores, is a wonderful concoction from the very north of Italy. A bit more brown in colour than regular polenta, it's made from a mix of buckwheat and corn, though the flavour is more nutty and less sweet than 100 per cent corn polenta. Buckwheat isn't as good a thickener as corn, so you'll need to add more polenta than you would for the more common variety. If you're using pure corn polenta, then use about two-thirds the amount.

Put 2 litres (70 fl oz/8 cups) water in a large saucepan and heat until it is almost boiling. Add the salt and sprinkle in the polenta, whisking constantly. The greatest risks are that the polenta will form lumps at this stage and the possibility of it burning towards the end. Bring the polenta back to the boil while stirring continuously with a wooden spoon. Reduce the heat to low and simmer, stirring and scraping the base of the pan occasionally, for about 45–60 minutes — it really does improve with time. If the mixture becomes too hard to stir as it thickens, add a little more water, particularly in the last 10 minutes, though don't add too much or the flavour will end up watery too. When done, the polenta should be just runny enough to be poured from the pan, but no runnier.

Stir in the butter and cheese until both have melted and season with salt and freshly ground black pepper. Serve immediately with a meat-based ragu such as the stout, beef shin and mushroom ragu, pictured, (see page 102), the duck and brussels sprout sauce (see page 116), the rabbit ragu (see page 94) or the lamb breasts with capers, tomato and anchovies (see page 134).

2 teaspoons salt
500 g (1 lb 2 oz/2⅔ cups) buckwheat polenta
100 g (3½ oz) butter
150 g (5½ oz) finely grated Italian parmesan cheese
meat-based ragu, to serve

White wine roasted chicken

serves 4

To me, picking over the bones of a great farmhouse chook is the perfect way to spend an evening in winter. The difference, perhaps, is that my chooks have grown slower and taste more of themselves than the chook most people can buy. Still, a good way to keep your free-range chicken moist right through is to cook it on its sides for a while.

Preheat the oven to 200°C (400°F/Gas 6). Rinse the chicken well and push some of the thyme under the skin, then fill the cavity with the remaining thyme and the bay leaves. Squeeze half of the lemon over the skin and place the squeezed half in the cavity. Push the butter up under the skin and rub the skin liberally with salt and freshly ground black pepper, perhaps using a light film of oil to help it stick.

Place the chicken on its side in a small roasting dish or tin and tip the wine into the dish. Add a few lemon slices and some more thyme, to taste. Roast the chicken on its side for 20 minutes, then turn and roast on the other side for a further 20 minutes. Turn the chicken, breast side up (legs sticking up in the air) and continue roasting for a further 20 minutes, or until the chicken is cooked. Check by inserting a knife between the thigh and body — there should be no pink juices or meat. A fan-forced grill (broiler) option on the oven is handy to brown the skin if it isn't already brown at this stage.

Remove from the oven, cover with foil and leave to rest for 10 minutes before carving and serving, using all that yummy juice in the bottom of the roasting dish as gravy.

2 kg (4 lb 8 oz) whole
  free-range chicken
3–4 thyme sprigs
2 bay leaves
1 lemon, halved
40 g (1½ oz) butter,
  softened
125 ml (4 fl oz/½ cup) dry
  white wine

Rib-sticking meals

Sticky beef ribs or rabbit ragu baked with fresh egg pasta. A sensational beef and stout pie in home-made puff pastry. If you can't have a goulash in winter, complete with sour cream and gherkins, when can you have it?

Slow-cooked meats are the order of the day during winter. Cured pork and sausages braised with cabbage in cider vinegar. Savoury mince under a thick doona of mash, enriched with cheddar and mustard. Slab bacon is scented with star anise in dishes where I let the oven do most of the work. Use these ideas as all recipes should be used — as a road map, not a set of instructions. Find your own way to your preferred destination. Use other cuts of meat — try venison shanks one day, goat the next. But whichever way you go, be sure to find a good book to bunker down with as the dishes spend time cooking.

Recipes

Cottage pie with mustard cheese topping

serves 8

The secret to making this cottage pie memorable is frying the onion to brown without burning it, and using good-quality beef mince, which doesn't mean lean. I don't add tomato paste to my cottage pie, letting the meat speak for itself. If you would like that rich tomato flavour, feel free to add some, but use it early and fry it for a couple of minutes with the meat.

To make the savoury mince, heat the butter in a large heavy-based frying pan over medium heat and cook the onion until it starts to brown. Add the meat, a little at a time, and cook for about 3–4 minutes — ideally you want the meat to brown without the onion burning, but usually mince is hard to colour because it sweats and boils before it has a chance to brown. It's more important to get the onions to brown than the meat in this dish, but if you can do both, even better. Add the thyme, bay leaf and worcestershire sauce and cook for 1–2 minutes, then pour in the stock and bring to the boil. Cover, reduce the heat to low, and simmer for at least 40 minutes, preferably 1 hour. Stir occasionally to stop it sticking to the pan and add a little more stock if it's getting too dry. Season with salt and freshly ground black pepper (remember the cheese in the mash on top is a little salty), then pour into a 2 litre (70 fl oz/8 cup) capacity casserole dish.

To make the potato topping, preheat the oven to 200°C (400°F/ Gas 6). Steam or boil the whole potatoes until tender. Drain, peel, then mash well. Add the cheese, butter, mustard and horseradish and stir to combine; some potatoes may need a little milk, but I usually don't bother.

Spread the mashed potato over the mince in the casserole dish and scrape the top with a fork or similar to get lots of peaks and troughs — these will caramelise during cooking and add more flavour. Bake the cottage pie in the centre of the oven for about 30 minutes, or until the pie is browned and starting to bubble up from the edges.

SAVOURY MINCE

50 g (1¾ oz) butter
3 large onions, finely diced
1 kg (2 lb 4 oz) minced (ground) beef
3 thyme sprigs
1 bay leaf
60 ml (2 fl oz/¼ cup) worcestershire sauce
500 ml (17 fl oz/2 cups) beef stock or water

POTATO TOPPING

1 kg (2 lb 4 oz) floury potatoes, such as kennebec
250 g (9 oz/2½ cups) grated cheddar cheese
100 g (3½ oz) butter
2 tablespoons English mustard
2 teaspoons grated horseradish, fresh if possible

Oven-baked pasta with rabbit ragu

There are plenty of ways to make a baked pasta, including using parboiled penne or spaghetti with a sauce. I've gone for flat lasagne-style pasta sheets with this rib-sticking rabbit ragu, which is probably as good as any sauce. If you don't want to make your own pasta, use instant lasagne sheets and simply moisten them first to ensure they cook through.

To make the rabbit ragu, preheat the oven to 180°C (350°F/Gas 4). Cut the rabbit into six portions — it doesn't need to be perfect as the meat will be taken off the bones. Remove the kidneys and the little sac of fat and finely chop them; they will add a delicious flavour. Season the rabbit with salt and freshly ground black pepper.

Heat the olive oil in a flameproof casserole dish over medium heat. Add the speck and cook for about 5 minutes, or until golden and any fat has rendered. Remove to a plate. Add half of the rabbit portions to the dish and cook them until brown on all sides — about 5–10 minutes. Remove to a plate and repeat with the remaining rabbit.

Reduce the heat to low and add the garlic to the dish, stirring to coat it with oil, then add the kidneys and their fat and cook for 3–4 minutes, being careful not to burn the garlic. Add the wine and, using a wooden spoon, scrape up any crusty bits stuck to the base of the dish — this is important for flavour. Add the tomato, rosemary and sage, and return the speck and rabbit portions to the dish. Stir well, cover, and bake in the oven for about 2 hours, or until the rabbit meat is falling off the bone. You may need to check halfway through cooking to see that it's not drying out and add some more water, wine or tomato if needed.

Remove the rabbit from the sauce and allow to cool slightly. Pull the meat from the bones using your fingers and chop any larger bits into bite-sized pieces. Return the meat to the sauce in the dish.

RABBIT RAGU
1.5 kg (3 lb 5 oz) rabbit
2 tablespoons olive oil, plus
  2 tablespoons extra
200 g (7 oz) speck, diced
2 garlic cloves, chopped
375 ml (13 fl oz/1½ cups)
  red wine
880 g (1 lb 15 oz/3½ cups)
  tinned chopped tomatoes
2 rosemary sprigs, chopped
2 sage sprigs, chopped
160 g (5¾ oz/2 cups) fresh
  sourdough breadcrumbs
1 small bunch flat-leaf
  (Italian) parsley, leaves
  chopped

continued...

Meanwhile, to make the pasta, mix together the eggs and flour in a bowl and then knead lightly, adding a little water or more flour as needed to give a dry but pliable dough. Roll through a pasta machine at its widest setting — you will need to put it through about ten times, folding once between each roll. This will knead the pasta far quicker and more effectively than if you do it by hand. Don't be afraid to use plenty of flour as you go because if the dough is too wet it will be too sticky to roll neatly. Once you've done this initial knead–roll, divide the dough into six portions and roll each portion through the machine, progressively reducing the settings until the second-last narrow setting on most pasta machines, where you roll it through twice. Cut the pasta to a shape to fit a 2 litre (70 fl oz/8 cup) capacity baking dish, bearing in mind that you will need three layers of pasta.

Drizzle 1 tablespoon of the extra olive oil in the base of the baking dish. Spread one-quarter of the rabbit ragu in the base of the dish in an even layer — don't smooth it out, you want a bumpy surface. Gently lay a sheet of pasta on top, poking it around the bumps of rabbit so it's not lying flat — you may have to use two or three pieces and overlap them slightly, depending on the shape of your baking dish. Continue layering until you have three layers of pasta and four layers of rabbit, finishing with a layer of rabbit.

In a medium-sized bowl mix together the breadcrumbs, most of the parsley and the remaining olive oil and toss to moisten the breadcrumbs. Scatter over the rabbit and bake in a 180°C (350°F/Gas 4) oven for about 30 minutes, or until the breadcrumbs are golden and the sauce is bubbling around the sides of the dish. Scatter the remaining parsley on top and serve.

FRESH PASTA
200 g (7 oz/1⅓ cups) plain
  (all-purpose) flour
2 eggs

Bratwurst with braised Lilliput lentils

serves 4

The small bluey green kind of lentil, the variety made famous by Puy in France and Castellucio in Italy, makes the perfect accompaniment for snags. Other lentils just don't work as well. Make a bigger batch and freeze the leftovers for mid-week meals.

To make the lentils, soak the mushrooms in 100 ml (3½ fl oz) boiling water until soft. Strain and reserve the liquid, squeezing out any excess water with your fingers. Slice the caps and set aside.

Heat the olive oil in a saucepan over medium heat and cook the speck for 3–4 minutes, or until the fat starts to melt out. Add the onion and carrot and cook for cook for 10 minutes, or until it softens and starts to colour slightly. Add the garlic and cook for 1 minute, then increase the heat and pour in the white wine. Bring to the boil for 1 minute, then add 1 litre (35 fl oz/4 cups) water, the lentils, thyme and bay leaf, and the reserved mushrooms and their liquid, and return to the boil. Reduce the heat to low and simmer for about 30 minutes, checking that the lentils remain just below the level of the liquid so they cook evenly. Put a lid on if you want. The lentils should be soft rather than crunchy, but not falling apart. When the lentils are just about done, increase the heat and boil rapidly to reduce the liquid until it's just a dribble to moisten the lentils. Season to taste with salt and freshly ground black pepper. Set aside and keep warm until ready to serve.

Meanwhile, cook the sausages in a chargrill pan or frying pan over medium–high heat for about 5–10 minutes, or until golden brown on the outside and cooked through. Serve immediately with the lentils on the side.

2–3 dried mushrooms, such as porcini or morels
1–2 tablespoons olive oil
100 g (3½ oz) speck, bacon or pancetta, cut into bite-sized pieces
1 onion, finely diced
1 small carrot, peeled and finely diced
1 garlic clove, crushed
2–3 tablespoons white wine
200 g (7 oz/1 cup) small Puy-style green lentils
2 thyme sprigs
1 bay leaf
4 big or 8 small bratwurst or other good-quality sausages

Pork and potato goulash

serves 5–6

This is a terrific dish that matches the wonderful flavour of slow-cooked pork with the bracing acidity of dill cucumbers and the richness of sour cream. If you don't have tomato passata, just blend or process tinned tomatoes in its place.

Preheat the oven to 150°C (300°F/Gas 2). Heat the olive oil in a large flameproof casserole dish over high heat. Dust the pork with the flour and cook the meat in batches until it's browned on all sides, rubbing the base of the dish with a wooden spoon to lift any stuck-on bits. Remove the meat to a plate.

Add the onion to the dish and cook over low heat for 5–10 minutes, or until softened and starting to colour, adding a touch more oil if necessary. Toss in the garlic and paprika and stir for 1 minute, then return the meat to the pan and add the tomato passata, salt, pepper and 500 ml (17 fl oz/ 2 cups) water, stirring well. Scrape the base of the dish, cover and bring to the boil.

Transfer the dish to the oven and bake for 1½ hours, giving it a stir halfway through cooking. Add the potatoes, pushing them into the liquid and bake until tender, at least another 30 minutes. Add the dill cucumbers and stir to combine. Stir in the sour cream, taste for seasoning, and serve with green vegetables and some sauerkraut, if you have any.

- 1–2 tablespoons olive oil or lard
- 1 kg (2 lb 4 oz) pork shoulder or similar, cut into large dice
- 1 tablespoon plain (all-purpose) flour
- 2 onions, thinly sliced
- 4 garlic cloves, sliced, crushed or just peeled
- 2 tablespoons sweet paprika
- 80 g (2¾ oz/⅓ cup) tomato passata (puréed tomatoes)
- 1 teaspoon salt
- ¼ teaspoon freshly ground black pepper
- 400 g (14 oz) baby potatoes, scrubbed, halved or quartered if large
- 80 g (2¾ oz) dill cucumbers (gherkins), chopped
- 100 g (3½ oz) sour cream

Stout, beef shin and mushroom pie

serves 8

It's better if you can cook the filling without using the flour — this creates a different textured filling but a more pleasant taste. I've included flour in the instructions to be sure that the filling isn't too wet. I also like to eat the filling with a baked potato or taragna (see page 83). This recipe uses an easy puff pastry perfect for a chunky winter pie or eccles cakes (see page 190). You can chill the butter in the freezer to make it easier to cut finely, and pop it into ice-cold water so you can keep each bit separate until you start to make the pastry.

To make the easy puff pastry, put the flour and salt into a large bowl and scatter in the butter. Tip in 170 ml (5½ fl oz/⅔ cup) chilled water, stirring with a spoon to combine. When it gets difficult to stir, use your hands to make a dough — don't worry if there are still some bits of butter not evenly incorporated; in fact, it's supposed to be that way. Roll the dough out on a well-floured work surface. Roll lengthways only to form a rectangle about 46 x 15 cm (18 x 6 inches). Fold the short edge over to one-third of the way towards the centre, then fold the other edge over the top to make a square. Viewed from the side, the pastry now has three layers. Cover with plastic wrap and refrigerate for 30 minutes.

Remove the dough from the refrigerator and turn it so that when you roll it out, it will be at right angles to the way it was before. Don't be afraid to use plenty of flour to stop the butter from sticking. Roll the pastry out again lengthways to form another 46 x 15 cm (18 x 6 inch) rectangle. Fold and wrap as before and rest in the refrigerator for a further 30 minutes. You may still be able to see flecks of butter in the pastry, and that's fine. Repeat this process twice more, ensuring that each time you rotate the dough by 90 degrees. Rest in the refrigerator until ready to use.

EASY PUFF PASTRY
270 g (9½ oz) plain (all-purpose) flour, sifted
a pinch of salt
200 g (7 oz) butter, chilled and cut into 5 mm (¼ inch) dice

continued...

To make the stout, beef and mushroom ragu, preheat the oven to 150°C (300°F/Gas 2). Heat 1 tablespoon of the oil in a large flameproof casserole dish over medium heat and cook the onion, carrot and celery for 10 minutes, or until they start to colour. Dust the beef with the flour and fry in the same dish, turning to brown the meat and adding more oil if necessary. Add the mushroom, bay leaves, thyme and stout and give a really good stir to loosen any bits stuck to the base of the dish. Bring to a simmer, stirring often, then add the garlic, salt and pepper. Cover and bake in the oven for 2 hours, or until the meat is tender. At this point you may need to put the dish on the stovetop again over high heat to reduce the sauce so it's quite thick. Allow to cool. Discard the bay leaf and thyme.

Increase the oven temperature to 180°C (350°F/Gas 4). Roll out two-thirds of the pastry to about 4 mm (⅛ inch) thick all over, large enough to line a 30 cm (12 inch) pie dish, allowing for a 1 cm (½ inch) overhang. Fill with the cooled beef mixture. Roll the remaining pastry into a circle large enough to cover the pie. Place it on top, pressing the edges together to seal. Brush the top with a little of the egg mixture and bake for about 50–60 minutes, or until the pie is golden.

Serve the pie hot with mashed spuds, a green vegetable of some kind and a stout to drink.

STOUT, BEEF AND MUSHROOM RAGU

2 tablespoons vegetable oil or 40 g (1½ oz) butter

1 onion, diced

1 carrot, diced

1 celery stalk, diced

1 kg (2 lb 4 oz) beef shin, roughly diced

1 tablespoon plain (all-purpose) flour

400 g (14 oz) mushrooms, sliced

2 bay leaves

2 thyme sprigs

200 ml (7 fl oz) stout or other dark beer

5 garlic cloves, peeled and sliced

1 teaspoon salt

½ teaspoon freshly ground black pepper

1 egg, lightly beaten with a pinch of salt

Braised cabbage with sausages and speck

serves 8

I wanted to cook a sausage and cabbage casserole, then suddenly realised I was doing a version of the classic Alsatian choucroute garnie (sauerkraut garnished with the meat it is cooked with). In the absence of sauerkraut in my neck of the woods, I decided to use fresh cabbage and a touch of vinegar. You can get a smoky flavour from hocks or bacon, and the Dutch rookworst-style sausage would also turn out wonderfully well.

Heat the lard in a large flameproof casserole dish with a tight-fitting lid over medium heat. Add the speck and sausages and cook for about 10 minutes, or until brown all over. Add the onion and continue cooking, stirring occasionally, until they have softened and have a bit of colour. Add the cabbage and continue cooking, with the lid on mostly, until it wilts. Sit the hock in a corner of the dish, add the juniper, bay leaves, wine and vinegar and bring to the boil. Add 500 ml (17 fl oz/2 cups) water, cover, reduce the heat to low and simmer for 1 hour.

Remove the lid, season with salt, to taste, then add the potatoes, pressing them into the liquid. When I do it, I turn over the hock and pull some of the sausages to the top to get the potatoes into that yummy cooking juice. Put the lid back on and cook for another 1–1½ hours.

Serve the cabbage and sauce with the meats, including the ham roughly pulled from the bone and the speck cut or pulled apart.

30 g (1 oz) lard or butter

100 g (3½ oz) speck or slab bacon

1 kg (2 lb 4 oz) pure pork sausages (I used Italian-style pork and fennel because I had some in the freezer)

2 large onions, sliced

1 kg (2 lb 4 oz) cabbage, shredded

400 g (14 oz) ham hock

10 juniper berries

3 bay leaves

250 ml (9 fl oz/1 cup) dry white wine

2½ tablespoons cider or wine vinegar

500 g (1 lb 2 oz) waxy potatoes, such as pink eyes, scrubbed and halved

Baked potatoes with savoury mince

serves 6

Preheat the oven to 200°C (400°F/Gas 6). Score the sides of the potatoes with a fork so that you break the skin. Stick a knife into each one to make sure it doesn't explode in the oven. Rub the potatoes well with salt and bake in the centre of the oven for about 1 hour, or until cooked. A good way to test is to insert a knife and make sure the innards are tender, or squeeze them to see if they feel soft right through.

Serve the potatoes on plates, cutting each one nearly in half and crossways again so that they fall open a little. You can push in from each quarter to fluff the potato a little. Dob with some butter or sour cream, if using, and serve the hot savoury mince on the side.

6 large baking potatoes, such as king edward, scrubbed
butter or sour cream, to serve, if you're up for it
1 quantity savoury mince (see page 93), heated

Food as humble as a monk and as noble as a prince.
Comfort food, that resonates with a sense of place.
Food that I remember from my childhood, only better.
Baked potatoes are the kind of food that fashion simply
never touches, which is a really good thing.

Pork chops baked with stout and mustard

serves 4

These chops, cooked to perfection with a sticky stout sauce spiked with mustard, are stonkingly good. Neck (forequarter) chops are less likely to dry out, especially if you're using any old pig, which, sadly, is what is most likely available. Serve with roast spuds, some boiled kale and carrots cooked with a hint of fennel seed.

Preheat the oven to 200°C (400°F/Gas 6). Heat the olive oil in a large frying pan over high heat and sear the chops to brown on both sides. Lay the chops in a roasting tin that fits them snugly in an even layer and season with a good amount of salt and freshly ground black pepper. Rub the garlic over the top.

Whisk together the mustard and stout in a bowl and spoon evenly over the surface of the chops. Using your fingers, rub the thyme leaves off the sprigs over the chops, then toss the sprigs in as well.

Cook the chops in the centre of the oven for about 25–30 minutes, turning them occasionally — you want the sauce to reduce and stick to the chops. If your pan is big or the chops are starting to catch, add a touch of water, and then baste the chops with the juices so they end up well smothered. Serve hot with any pan juices spooned over the top.

1 tablespoon olive oil or lard
4 x 2 cm (¾ inch) thick pork loin or forequarter chops
4 garlic cloves, crushed
3 tablespoons French-style mustard
125 ml (4 fl oz/½ cup) stout or other dark beer
2–3 thyme sprigs

Duck and brussels sprout sauce (with polenta, potatoes or pasta)

serves 4

I plucked some gorgeous young brussels sprouts off a bush in my vegie garden for the first time ever and they lifted my duck ragu on soft polenta to another level. The leftovers went just as well on pasta and a baked spud. If you have duck confit, or braised duck you can use that instead.

Preheat the oven to 180°C (350°F/Gas 4).

Put the duck, breast side down, in a shallow roasting tin. Add the wine and 250 ml (9 fl oz/1 cup) water. Roast in the oven for 1 hour, then turn it over, season with salt and freshly ground black pepper and cover the tin with foil. Return to the oven for a further 1 hour, making sure the tin doesn't dry out, because you want the juices to make a sauce.

Remove the duck from the oven and drain the juices into a cup or bowl. Scrape up any bits from the base of the tin and add those to the cup too. Refrigerate to cool; as the juices cool the fat will rise to the surface so you can remove it more easily (this can be used later to bake potatoes or to fry the brussels sprouts in).

When the duck is cool enough to handle, pull the meat from the carcass and shred into bite-sized pieces. Put in a saucepan over medium heat, along with the sauce (minus the fat), the sage leaves and the butter. Simmer for 3–4 minutes, adding a little water if the sauce is looking too dry, until heated through.

Heat the lard in a large frying pan over medium heat and cook the garlic until it just starts to sizzle. Add the brussels sprouts, increase the heat, and cook until the leaves are lightly crisp — you may need to add more lard.

You can serve the meat over taragna (see page 83), with baked potatoes (see page 111) or even tossed through a lovely fresh pasta, and crown with the fried brussels sprouts.

1.6 kg (3 lb 8 oz) whole duck or 4 duck leg quarters

250 ml (9 fl oz/1 cup) red wine

6 sage leaves, roughly torn

20 g (¾ oz) butter

1–2 tablespoons lard

2 garlic cloves, sliced

200 g (7 oz) brussels sprouts, thinly sliced lengthways

Pot-roast quail with pomegranate

serves 8

When you can't get pomegranates (which is often) use pomegranate molasses, a fabulous syrup which keeps for ages.

Preheat the oven to 160°C (315°F/Gas 2–3).

Heat the olive oil in a large flameproof casserole dish or cast-iron pot that is big enough to hold the quails in a single layer, over medium heat. Season the quails with salt and freshly ground black pepper and cook to brown on all sides. Remove to a plate and keep warm.

Remove most of the oil from the dish and cook the onion and garlic for 5 minutes, or until softened. Add the tomato and cook for 5 minutes, stirring regularly. Add the wine, bring to the boil and cook until the liquid has reduced by one-third. Add the pomegranate juice (or pomegranate molasses mixture) and the pomegranate seeds.

Return the quails to the dish, arranging them in a single layer, breast side down. Add enough of the stock to barely cover (don't worry if they're a little exposed). Season with salt and freshly ground black pepper, cover, and cook in the oven for about 35 minutes, or until nicely cooked through yet moist. Remove from the oven and allow to rest for 15 minutes before adjusting the seasoning to taste. Serve with Turkish-style pide bread and a green salad.

2–3 tablespoons olive oil

8 quails, rinsed and patted dry

1 onion, finely chopped

2 garlic cloves, finely chopped

4 ripe tomatoes, finely chopped

100 ml (3½ fl oz) white wine

juice of 2 pomegranates or use 1 tablespoon pomegranate molasses in 250 ml (9 fl oz/1 cup) water

1 tablespoon pomegranate seeds, slightly crushed

150 ml (5 fl oz) roasted chicken stock (see page 54)

Sticky beef ribs

serves 4

This is a marvellous way to use up beef ribs. The meat from some ribs can be a bit chewy, so you could simmer them for an hour or so before marinating them to make them more tender and render out more of the fat. (Alternatively, cook them lower and slower in the oven, perhaps covering for the first hour with foil.) The idea is to reduce the marinade onto the bones and meat as it cooks, so when they're finished, they're dark and slightly sweet and tart from the tamarind. For this I used a tamarind pulp concentrate with the consistency of pouring cream. It's easier to use than the paste, though you could try that too.

Combine all of the ingredients, except the ribs, in a large non-metallic bowl and mix well to combine. Add the ribs and use your hands to toss and coat the ribs. Cover with plastic wrap and refrigerate overnight.

Remove the ribs from the refrigerator about 1 hour before cooking and preheat the oven to 180°C (350°F/Gas 4). Remove the ribs (reserving the marinade) and spread out in a lightly oiled roasting tin and roast for 1 hour. Turn the ribs over, pour over any remaining marinade, and cook for a further 1 hour, or until the ribs are dark and sticky — you can add 1 tablespoon water to the base of the tin and baste the ribs occasionally to get even more flavour. Ideally, the marinade will caramelise onto the ribs rather than the tin, so the more basting, the better. You can serve the ribs with steamed rice and caramelised brussels sprouts colcannon (see page 167).

250 ml (9 fl oz/1 cup) tamarind pulp concentrate

60 ml (2 fl oz/¼ cup) olive oil, plus extra, for greasing

60 ml (2 fl oz/¼ cup) dark soy sauce

4 garlic cloves, crushed

finely grated zest of 1 orange

7–8 star anise

1 tablespoon finely grated fresh ginger

1 tablespoon maple syrup or soft brown sugar

1 teaspoon ground cardamom

1 teaspoon ground fennel

1 teaspoon salt

8 beef ribs (you will probably have to order ahead from your butcher)

Chicken tagine with green olives and quince

serves 4

Many people use honey to give their tagine some sweetness, but I find I prefer to save the sweetness for dessert. In place of the oft-used dates, I've gone for quinces because you can still get them in early winter where I live and their fragrance gives the tagine a real lift.

Preheat the oven to 160°C (315°F/Gas 2–3).

Heat the olive oil in a large flameproof casserole dish with a tight-fitting lid, over medium heat. Add the chicken and brown on both sides. Remove to a plate.

In the same dish, cook the onion for 6–8 minutes, or until lightly caramelised, then stir in the garlic and cook for a further 1 minute. Reduce the heat to low, add the cinnamon, cumin, coriander and cloves, and cook for 1 minute, stirring a little, until fragrant.

Add 250 ml (9 fl oz/1 cup) water to the dish, scrape up any bits stuck to the base, then return the chicken to the sauce. Add the olives and quince, cover and bake in the oven for about 1½ hours, or until the quince and chicken are tender. Add the lemon slices, season with salt and freshly ground black pepper, to taste (I do it now because the olives are salty), and cook for another 10 minutes with the lid off. Serve immediately with rice or couscous.

2 tablespoons olive oil
4 chicken leg quarters
2 large onions, diced
4 garlic cloves, crushed
1 cinnamon stick
¼ teaspoon ground cumin
¼ teaspoon ground coriander
a pinch of ground cloves
12 good-quality large green olives
1 large quince, peeled, cored and cut into 3 cm (1¼ inch) pieces
3 thin lemon slices (or the rind from ¼ preserved lemon)

Not your ordinary meatloaf

serves 8

Until recently meatloaf, to me, meant a bloke with huge lungs and a great album from the 1970s. I had only eaten it (the dinner version) a couple of times, and didn't really like it. Then a friend made a terrine and I thought that meatloaf really should be a thing of beauty. This is my version. It may look like a long list of ingredients, but most should already be in the cupboard.

Preheat the oven to 200°C (400°F/Gas 6).

Heat the olive oil in a large frying pan over medium heat. Add the onion, thyme and bacon and cook, covered, for about 5 minutes, or until the onion is very soft, stirring often. Remove from the heat and allow to cool.

Transfer the bacon mixture to a bowl and add the remaining ingredients, using your hands to mix everything together. Press the mixture into a 1.5 litre (52 fl oz/6 cup) capacity casserole dish or loaf (bar) tin. Place the dish in a larger roasting tin and pour in enough boiling water to come at least 3 cm (1¼ inches) up the sides of the dish. This isn't essential, but I think it makes the end texture better. Bake for 50–60 minutes, or until a fork inserted in the centre comes out warm, and there are no more pink juices (it won't hurt if it's slightly underdone). Serve the meatloaf hot, with baked potatoes and leftovers at room temperature, with plenty of mustard.

2 tablespoons olive oil or 40 g (1½ oz) butter

1 large onion, finely diced

5 thyme sprigs, leaves stripped from stem if woody

2 bacon slices, finely diced

600 g (1 lb 5 oz) minced (ground) veal or beef (not lean)

400 g (14 oz) minced (ground) pork (not lean)

60 g (2¼ oz/¼ cup) tomato passata (puréed tomatoes)

2 eggs

100 g (3½ oz/1¼ cups) fresh breadcrumbs

2 tablespoons dijon mustard, plus extra, to serve

1 teaspoon salt

½ teaspoon freshly ground black pepper

50 g (1¾ oz/⅓ cup) finely grated Italian parmesan cheese

Pork and black bean stew

serves 6

There are many pork and black bean dishes from the Americas, although this probably isn't one. It's simply my take on a hearty, porky stew using creamy textured black beans. Good pork will make this sing. If you can't get full-flavoured free-range pork, add a little diced carrot and celery to the sautéed onion and serve some sour cream on the table to stir through. Pure pork sausages also work well and if you're using lots of cured meats and bacon rather than fresh, cut down on the amount to allow for their intense flavour.

Put the black beans in a large saucepan with the whole onion, whole garlic cloves, bay leaves and thyme. Cover with plenty of water, bring to the boil and simmer for about 1–1½ hours, or until tender, but not completely mushy — the time will depend on the beans, their age and how long they soak. Drain well, reserving the cooking liquid and discarding the onion, garlic, bay leaves and thyme.

Heat the lard in a large saucepan over high heat and cook the pork until it starts to brown. Add the diced onion and continue to cook until it starts to colour. Add the chilli, crushed garlic and cumin seeds and cook for another 1–2 minutes, stirring constantly. Add the black beans and their cooking liquid and top up with water if needed to create a stew rather than soup consistency. (In other words, just cover the beans, don't drown them.) Season with salt and freshly ground black pepper and simmer for 30 minutes, or until the beans become creamy. Serve the pork and black bean stew with steamed basmati rice and yoghurt on the side.

Variations: You can purée one-third of the beans after their first cooking to give the stew a creamier consistency. This dish can also be finished by cooking it in a low oven, rather than on the stovetop for the last 30 minutes — this will give it a different consistency, and means you can cook it drier.

500 g (1 lb 2 oz/2¼ cups) dried black beans, soaked overnight, rinsed and drained

3 onions, 1 peeled and left whole and 2 diced

4 garlic cloves, 2 peeled and left whole and 2 crushed

2 bay leaves

1 thyme sprig

2 tablespoons lard or 40 g (1½ oz) butter

500 g (1 lb 2 oz) pork, be it diced shoulder meat, cured belly, pure pork sausages, bacon or even better, a mix of cuts

1–2 bird's eye chillies, seeded and chopped

2 teaspoons cumin seeds

Cider-cooked bacon with star anise

serves 8

I just adore good bacon, one that has been put in a smoker (most these days haven't, just so you know), with its dark rind and deep flavour. Here I use it to make a meat course for dinner, matching the brightness and integrity of farmhouse cider with the liquorice notes of anise. If you can't get good cider, use a commercial drop enhanced with about 10 per cent cloudy apple juice and a splash of cider vinegar to get a truer apple flavour.

Preheat the oven to 140°C (275°F/Gas 1).

Place the bacon, skin side up, in a small roasting tin and tip enough cider over to barely cover. Add the star anise and garlic and push them down beside the bacon. Cover with foil and bake for about 3 hours, or until the meat is tender. Serve chunks of the bacon with your favourite winter vegetables (see pages 144–171).

1 kg (2 lb 4 oz) smoked bacon slab
750 ml (26 fl oz/3 cups) good-quality apple cider
2 star anise
2 garlic cloves, peeled

If I lived amongst vines, I'd cook a lot more with wine.
If we grew a lot of plums then I might make plum wine,
or dry them and use more prunes. But I live amongst
orchards and cider is the drink on many a smallholder's lips.

Sicilian-style braised lamb shoulder with wild fennel and potato

serves 6

I heard about this dish from a Sicilian visitor to the farm. It sounded so good I made it with my own Wiltshire Horn lamb and wild fennel from my mate Ross's place. I don't know if it tastes like the original, but it sure tastes good.

Put the lamb into a large flameproof casserole dish or cast-iron pot with a tight-fitting lid. Add the fennel tops, garlic bulbs, onion, salt, pepper and 1 litre (35 fl oz/4 cups) water. Cover and place over high heat until it just starts to simmer, then reduce the heat to low and simmer for 2 hours. When the meat is near enough to tender, push the potatoes down into the cooking juices and continue cooking for a further 1 hour. At this point it may be nice to cool the dish overnight and skim off the fat before reheating and eating. If you're in a hurry, skim off any of the liquid fat and eat the same day.

1.5 kg (3 lb 5 oz) lamb shoulder, boned, trimmed of fat, cut into roughly 6 cm (2½ inch) square chunks

1 big handful wild fennel tops, or use cultivated if need be

2 whole garlic bulbs, halved through the middle

4 large onions, diced

2 teaspoons salt

½ teaspoon freshly ground black pepper

1 kg (2 lb 4 oz) waxy potatoes, such as Dutch cream, scrubbed and quartered

Lamb breasts with capers, tomato and anchovies

serves 6

Often discarded by butchers, the belly (breast/flap) of lamb is streaked with fat and connective tissue, but also packed with flavour. In winter you can simply cook it down on the bone until the meat is easily separated from the other bits, then find any number of uses for the resultant intense meaty sauce. Try it in place of the rabbit with the oven-baked pasta (see page 94), or over baked potatoes (see page 111) or with taragna (see page 83). You can always substitute lamb shoulder (though it has more meat than the breasts, so adjust the amount used accordingly).

Preheat the oven to 150°C (300°F/Gas 2).

Put the lamb into a large ovenproof saucepan with a tight-fitting lid and add the remaining ingredients and 125 ml (4 fl oz/½ cup) water. Cover and bake for 3 hours, checking from time to time that it isn't drying out and adding more water if needed.

When the meat is falling from the bone, set aside until it is cool enough to handle. Strip the meat away from the bone and set aside. Refrigerate the sauce for 2–3 hours so you can scoop off the solidified fat — unless you want to eat this kind of fat, which I tend not to.

Mix the meat back through the sauce, reheat and serve with baked potatoes, on polenta or with a little pilaf rice, or through pasta dishes, using a little pasta cooking water if necessary to help moisten it, and just a hint of grated pecorino cheese on top.

2 kg (4 lb 8 oz) lamb breasts (flaps)

400 g (14 oz) tinned chopped tomatoes

50 g (1¾ oz) salted capers, rinsed

4 anchovy fillets, roughly chopped

10 garlic cloves, peeled

2 onions, diced

125 ml (4 fl oz/½ cup) white wine

Casserole chicken with white wine, mushrooms and sage

serves 3–4

This dish is best cooked on the bone, though you can cook it with or without the skin. It's an excellent way to use the more robust flavoured chicken thighs, rather than breast.

Preheat the oven to 150°C (300°F/Gas 2).

Heat the butter in a large flameproof casserole dish with a tight-fitting lid over medium heat. Dust the chicken lightly with the flour (an easy way to do this is to put them both in a plastic bag and shake well). Cook the chicken for about 5 minutes, or until just golden on both sides — you may need to do this in two batches, adding a touch more butter if necessary. Remove the chicken to a plate.

Reduce the heat to low, add the leek to the dish and cook for about 8–10 minutes, or until softened but not brown. Return the chicken to the dish, add the wine and simmer for 1–2 minutes. Toss in the mushrooms, then two-thirds of the sage, and season with salt and freshly ground black pepper. Cover and cook in the oven for about 1 hour, or until the chicken is tender and comes easily from the bone. Throw in the remaining sage, taste for seasoning, and serve with boiled potatoes or slices of crusty chargrilled bread.

25 g (1 oz) butter

1 kg (2 lb 4 oz/about 8) chicken thighs

2 tablespoons plain (all-purpose) flour, for dusting

1 leek, white part only, rinsed and chopped

250 ml (9 fl oz/1 cup) dry white wine

200 g (7 oz) button mushrooms

15 large sage leaves, torn

Corned beef with horseradish sauce

serves 8

If you're going to cook corned beef, you may as well cook a lot, enough for a large family. Use the leftovers for other meals or in the corned beef hash for brunch (see page 20). When making the horseradish sauce use the corned beef cooking liquid to give it a nicer edge than using milk alone. The amount of horseradish you need may vary depending on the type and brand you can get. Let your sense of taste be the guide.

To cook the silverside, put all of the ingredients into a large saucepan that is big enough to hold the beef with a few centimetres spare at the top. Fill the pan with cold water so it just covers the beef and place over high heat. Bring to the boil, then reduce the heat to low and simmer, partially covered, for 4 hours (barely simmering is better than bubbling madly). If you have an oven that is on, the beef also loves the gentle heat of a slow cooling oven. Drain the meat, reserving the cooking liquid for the sauce and to cook your spuds in, set aside the onions and carrots and discard the spices.

To make the horseradish sauce, put the milk, cloves, onion and corned beef cooking liquid in a saucepan over high heat until nearly boiling. Turn off the heat and allow to steep for 15 minutes. Strain.

Heat the butter in a small saucepan and then toss in the flour, stirring to make a paste. Cook for 1 minute or so, then whisk in the milk. Keep whisking as it comes to the boil and thickens. If you can't whisk out the lumps, strain first, then stir in the mustard and horseradish. Season with salt and pepper, to taste. It's unlikely you'll need more salt because the beef cooking liquid is salty. Add more beef cooking liquid if it's too thick, cover by pressing with plastic wrap so it doesn't get a skin on it.

Serve the silverside cut into large chunks with the carrots and onions and the horseradish sauce on the side.

2 kg (4 lb 8 oz) corned silverside
10 juniper berries
2 large onions, unpeeled and left whole
2 carrots, halved
celery tops and parsley stalks, if you have them
2 tablespoons red or white wine vinegar
3 bay leaves

HORSERADISH SAUCE
250 ml (9 fl oz/1 cup) milk
2 whole cloves
½ onion, peeled
250 ml (9 fl oz/1 cup) corned beef cooking liquid
20 g (¾ oz) butter
1 tablespoon plain (all-purpose) flour
1 tablespoon dijon mustard
2 tablespoons creamed horseradish, or to taste

Ross's twice-cooked pork shoulder

serves 8

This recipe, kindly shared by my mate Ross O'Meara, is pork cooking for dummies; the meat is already tender and moist from slow cooking, then all you have to aim for is crackling. There's no risk of dry overcooked meat or a raw middle. What's more, it tastes incredible.

To make the pork stock, put all of the ingredients into a stockpot or large saucepan and check that the bones are covered. Press them down if need be and then place over high heat and bring to the boil. Reduce the heat to low and simmer for about 8 hours, topping up with water occasionally so the liquid level doesn't drop below the level of the bones. Ideally, the skin of the hocks will be starting to break down completely. Strain and discard the solids and keep the broth — you should have about 4 litres (140 fl oz).

Preheat the oven to 120°C (235°F/Gas ½). Put the pork shoulder, skin side up, into a large flameproof casserole dish with a tight-fitting lid. Add the stock and salt — the liquid won't cover the meat, and that's fine, though you may want to cook it for a while, skin side down, at the start to even out the cooking. Bring to the boil, then reduce the heat, cover, and place in the oven for 3–4 hours. You want the meat to be very tender, but not so soft that it falls apart. Remove from the oven and cool on the bench, then remove from the stock. (The stock is re-usable and makes excellent risotto and noodle soups.) Allow the meat to stand, uncovered, overnight in the refrigerator to dry out the skin.

PORK STOCK
4 raw pork hocks
1 set pork ribs, cut to fit the pot
2 brown onions, halved
1 garlic bulb
3 bay leaves
1 thyme sprig
additional piece pork skin, if available
6 litres (210 fl oz) water

3 kg (6 lb 12 oz) pork shoulder, boned and skin on
2 tablespoons salt
1 kg (1 lb 2 oz) waxy potatoes, such as Dutch cream
4 red onions, sliced
olive oil, for rubbing on

continued...

When ready to cook the second time, remove the pork from the refrigerator. Preheat the oven to 230°C (450°F/Gas 8). Wash and slice all of the potatoes about 5 mm (¼ inch) thick and lay in the base of a large roasting tin with the onion slices. Put the pork on top, skin side up. Score the fat as you would for a normal roast; lines through the fat but not into the flesh, about 1.5 cm (⅝ inch) apart. Season the skin well with fine table salt and a little freshly ground black pepper, rubbed on with a light oil to help the seasoning stick. Roast the pork for roughly 30 minutes to crisp the skin. Turn the tray around to get the meat to cook evenly. (If the potatoes are becoming too dry, use some of the pork cooking liquid to moisten them.)

Continue to roast for another 20–30 minutes to heat the meat through, perhaps dropping the temperature of the oven to 180°C (350°F/Gas 4) if and when the skin has crackled sufficiently.

Remove the crackling to carve the meat and serve fat slices of the meat with the crackling, with some of the juice as a sauce.

Winter vegetables

It's a rare person who thinks of cabbage as sexy. Unless it's wilted with bacon and mustard. How about cauliflower? Fried to tan then dressed with chickpea aïoli. Beetroot? No problem when it's drenched with blue cheese sauce.

Winter vegetables can get a bad wrap. The thing is, they aren't as shallow as summer vegetables. Blanch brussels sprouts like you would peas and they're hard to love, tossed in a stir-fry like sugar snaps and you'll be disappointed, but cooked to dark on one side and stirred through chunky mashed potatoes and you've got something special. Roast the most ordinary of brown onions until they caramelise and bake them into a goat's cheese custard and you've created a meal.

Kale, broccoli, cabbage and their ilk make sense when you live seasonally. They thrive in the cooler months and their gentle bitterness can be the perfect foil for slow-braised meats. All those beans, peas and other greens can wait until summer.

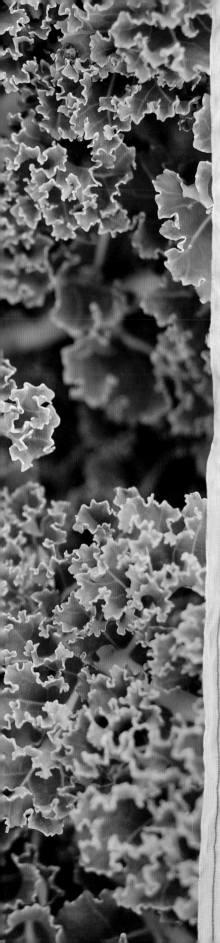

Recipes

Wilted cabbage, garlic and bacon with hot English mustard

serves 4

I got the idea for this dish from a visitor to my website, though I'm not sure it was winter where he was when he cooked it (Papua New Guinea, from memory). The spicy nature of the mustard is wonderful with the cabbage, but you may want to use dijon or similar if you don't want the pungency. The dish is wonderful in its own right, though you could serve it as a side dish to a meat and use less bacon.

Cut the cabbage into thick slices, then into 2–3 cm (¾–1¼ inch) squares. Rinse under cold water and drain in a colander.

Heat the olive oil in a large frying pan with a tight-fitting lid over medium heat. Add the bacon and cook for 5 minutes, or until golden brown. Reduce the heat, add the garlic and stir for 1 minute.

Add the cabbage with any water still attached to the leaves and toss thoroughly to coat in the bacon mixture. Increase the heat until it starts to sizzle, then reduce the heat, cover, and cook for 5 minutes, or until the underside is starting to turn golden on the edges. Give the cabbage a toss, replace the lid and allow to cook for a further 5 minutes, then stir in the mustard and cook for another 1 minute to heat through. Taste for mustard and season with a little salt before serving.

½ cabbage
2 tablespoons olive oil
300 g (10½ oz) thick bacon or speck, cut into strips
2 garlic cloves, finely chopped
1–2 tablespoons hot English mustard

Caramelised parsnips with feta

serves 6

This wonderful winter vegetable is given a hint of sweetness (though I like to turn it almost bitter in the oven) from the sugar and butter, before being paired with salty feta in a love match of flavours.

Preheat the oven to 220°C (425°F/Gas 7). Put the parsnips in a roasting tin and toss with enough olive oil to coat lightly; season with salt and freshly ground black pepper.

Roast the parsnips in the centre of the oven for 40–50 minutes, turning every now and then, so they brown nicely. When light brown on a couple of sides, toss with the butter and sprinkle with the sugar and continue cooking to caramelise the sugar.

Put the parsnips on a big platter, sprinkle with the feta and parsley and serve immediately.

2 kg (4 lb 8 oz) parsnips, peeled, trimmed, halved or quartered lengthways
1–2 tablespoons olive oil
20–40 g (¾–1½ oz) butter
2 teaspoons sugar
100 g (3½ oz) good-quality feta cheese, crumbled
chopped flat-leaf (Italian) parsley, to serve (optional)

There are treasures buried in the garden. The fully formed parsnips and beetroot lie in wait, doing little as the sun barely scrapes the garden's surface. Though they're not growing, they hold well in the dark, rich soil, waiting for their moment of glory in the winter kitchen.

Paprika braised chickpeas with kale

serves 6

This thick vegetarian stew can also be eaten with smoked paprika replacing 1 teaspoon of sweet paprika, and a rouille or spicy garlic mayonnaise dolloped over the hot stew at the end.

Put the chickpeas in a large saucepan, cover with water and simmer for 1 hour, or until they are just starting to become tender, but not cooked through. Drain well, reserving the cooking liquid and set aside. Strip the soft green part from above the ribs of the kale leaves and set aside.

Heat the olive oil in a large saucepan over medium heat. Add the onion, bay leaves and cinnamon and cook for 10–15 minutes, or until the onion starts to brown. Add the garlic and cook for 1 minute, then reduce the heat, add the paprika and cumin and cook for 30 seconds, stirring constantly and being careful not to scorch the spices. Add the tomato, kale and 500 ml (17 fl oz/2 cups) water and stir to combine.

Add the chickpeas and salt to the pan with just enough of the reserved cooking liquid to cover. Bring to the boil, then reduce the heat to low, cover and simmer for 1 hour, or until the chickpeas are buttery soft. Alternatively, you can cook this dish in a 140°C (275°F/Gas 1) oven for 2 hours.

Just before serving, season with salt and freshly ground black pepper and stir in the extra virgin olive oil. Serve warm with steamed rice or Turkish bread.

500 g (1 lb 2 oz/2½ cups) dried chickpeas, soaked overnight, rinsed and drained

10 large red Russian kale leaves or cavolo nero or silverbeet

1 tablespoon olive oil

3 large onions, diced

2 bay leaves

1 small piece cinnamon stick

6 garlic cloves, roughly chopped

3 teaspoons sweet paprika

1 teaspoon ground cumin

400 g (14 oz) tinned chopped tomatoes

1 teaspoon salt

2 tablespoons extra virgin olive oil

Roasted beetroot with blue cheese dressing

serves 4

Darkly roasted beets come up a treat with the sparkling acidity of blue cheese cut with cream. Would you eat this marvellous dish in summer? I think not.

Preheat the oven to 220°C (425°F/Gas 7). Put the beetroot in a roasting tin and coat with just enough olive oil so that they glisten; season well with salt and freshly ground black pepper. Roast towards the top of the oven for 40–50 minutes, turning occasionally, until nicely coloured and just tender.

While the beetroot roasts, make the dressing. Heat the cream in a small saucepan over low heat and add the cheese, stirring until it melts and adding more cream if the sauce is too thick.

Serve the beetroot on a platter and dress with the sauce, or put them separately on the table and let people help themselves.

2 large beetroot (beets), scrubbed and cut into eighths
olive oil, for drizzling
80 ml (2½ fl oz/⅓ cup) pouring (whipping) cream
60 g (2¼ oz) blue cheese, such as stilton or Roquefort, crumbled or chopped

Roasted onions and goat's cheese baked custard

serves 6

Because farmhouse goat's cheese is harder to come by in winter (they don't milk the goats in the cooler months), you can use a vacuum-packed cheese in this wonderful vegetarian dish.

Preheat the oven to 220°C (425°F/Gas 7). Quarter the onions without peeling them or cutting off the root end — this way they'll hold together much better. Now peel each quarter carefully. Place in a roasting tin, drizzle over a little olive oil and toss gently to coat. Scatter with thyme and season with salt and freshly ground black pepper. Roast the onions for about 45–60 minutes, or until quite dark but not burnt, then remove from the oven.

   Reduce the oven temperature to 180°C (350°F/Gas 4). Lay the onions in a 1.25 litre (44 fl oz/5 cup) capacity round baking dish or similar. Whisk the eggs in a large bowl, then whisk in the milk; season well. Pour into the dish over the onion and dot the cheese around. Bake in the oven for 30–40 minutes, or until the custard is set. Serve warm or at room temperature.

6 large onions
2 thyme sprigs
olive oil, for drizzling
10 eggs
1 litre (35 fl oz/4 cups) milk
**200 g (7 oz) soft goat's
  cheese**

Winter vegetables

Artichokes with mustard dipping sauce

serves 4

While artichokes — a flower — are more likely to be recognised as a spring vegetable, the first of the crop is often found in late winter. Forget the cutting and mucking around to get to the heart, just cook them whole, enjoy a lot more free time and have more fun at the dinner table.

Give the artichokes a good rinse and put them into a large saucepan, squeezing them in beside each other. Add enough water to cover the artichokes, about 2 litres (70 fl oz/8 cups), along with the bay leaves, lemon, thyme, garlic, olive oil and salt, and season with freshly ground black pepper. Place over high heat, cover and bring to the boil. Reduce the heat to low and simmer for about 20 minutes, or until the artichokes are tender. You can tell they're tender by inserting a knife into the centre and feeling for resistance. When they're ready you can let them cool in this liquid or you can pull them out straight away.

To make the mustard dipping sauce, whisk the mustard in a bowl, adding the olive oil gradually to make a nice dipping consistency. Add the spring onion, if using.

Serve the artichokes in a big bowl on the table with an even bigger empty bowl for the scraps. Give each person a little dipping bowl of mustard sauce. Guests pull leaves from the artichokes and dip the base of each leaf in the sauce. You simply run your teeth along the leaf to pull off any tender artichoke, which will become easier the further into the flower you go. Eventually, you'll be left with the heart and the choke. Scoop the choke out with a teaspoon and discard it, then enjoy the heart.

16 small young globe
  artichokes with firm heads
2 bay leaves
1 lemon, halved
2 thyme sprigs
6 garlic cloves, bruised
2 tablespoons olive oil
2 teaspoons salt

**MUSTARD DIPPING
  SAUCE**
3 tablespoons dijon mustard
2 tablespoons extra virgin
  olive oil
1 spring onion (scallion),
  white part only, thinly
  sliced (optional)

Jansson's temptation

This is inspired by a Swedish dish that takes the humble potato and makes it worthy of desire. You can replace all or part of the milk with cream, and perhaps top it with breadcrumbs if you like.

Preheat the oven to 180°C (350°F/Gas 4).

Heat the butter in a large flameproof casserole dish with a tight-fitting lid over medium–high heat. Add the onion and cook for 5–7 minutes, or until softened but not coloured. Add the garlic and cook for 1 minute, then add the potato and anchovy and toss well to combine. Press down on the potato to compact it a little, then add enough milk to barely come to the top of the potato. Cover and cook in the oven for 40 minutes, then remove the lid and bake for a further 40 minutes, or until the potato is tender.

40 g (1½ oz) butter
2 large onions, thinly sliced
2 garlic cloves, crushed
1 kg (2 lb 4 oz) waxy potatoes, such as Dutch cream, peeled and cut into round slices, about 5 mm (¼ inch) thick
5–6 anchovy fillets, roughly chopped
375 ml (13 fl oz/1½ cups) milk

Caramelised brussels sprout colcannon

serves 4

The trick to perfecting this dish is to get one side of the brussels really nicely caramelised for maximum flavour. If you want, you can substitute good olive oil for the butter and omit the milk, and simply swizzle the spuds in the pan and fry them for a bit.

Steam or boil the potatoes until tender. Drain well.

Meanwhile, heat the lard in a large heavy-based frying pan with a tight-fitting lid over medium heat. Place the brussels sprouts, cut side down, in a single layer in the base of the pan (this will help to brown the underside of each sprout). Cover and let the sprouts steam from the top and fry from the bottom.

Coarsely crush the hot potato with the milk, add the brussels sprouts and season with salt and lots of freshly ground black pepper.

Serve with sticky beef ribs (see page 119) or Ross's twice-cooked pork shoulder (see page 140).

500 g (1 lb 2 oz) waxy potatoes, such as nicola or Dutch cream, peeled
50 g (1¾ oz) lard or butter
500 g (1 lb 2 oz) brussels sprouts, cut in half lengthways
60 ml (2 fl oz/¼ cup) milk, or a mixture of milk and pouring (whipping) cream

It came as a surprise to me that the very top of my brussels sprouts, the volleyball-shaped leaves atop the stem (the stem is where the sprouts pop out) are also edible. At the end of the season you can lop this off and cook it as you would cabbage. Try frying it with garlic and olive oil or adding to any meaty braise. You could also throw it into the chickpeas in place of kale (see page 155) or give it a go in the cabbage braise (see page 149).

Fried cauliflower with chickpea aïoli

serves 4

The flavour of cauliflower becomes completely different when it's fried or roasted to deep brown, as it is cooked in parts of the eastern Mediterranean. This is a wonderful way to snack on a great winter vegetable.

To make the chickpea aïoli, put the chickpeas, egg yolk, lemon juice, mustard and garlic in a food processor and process to make a smooth purée. Combine both of the olive oils and with the motor running, add the oil in a steady stream to emulsify. Add salt and freshly ground black pepper to make the aïoli zappy enough for your tastes, and lick a bit off your fingers to really appreciate it.

Line a couple of trays with paper towels, ready to drain the cauliflower florets once cooked. Pour enough olive oil into a saucepan or wok so it is about 3 mm (⅛ inch) deep. Heat the oil over high heat and fry the cauliflower, in batches, turning them often to brown on as many sides as possible — they should be a deep golden, almost turning to dark brown. Drain on the paper towels as you go, and add more oil to the pan as necessary. Alternatively, you can deep-fry the cauliflower.

Serve the cauliflower warm or at room temperature with the chickpea aïoli and lemon wedges on the side for everyone to help themselves.

CHICKPEA AÏOLI
100 g (3½ oz) cooked chickpeas (tinned are okay), rinsed and drained
1 egg yolk
2 teaspoons freshly squeezed lemon juice or wine vinegar
1 teaspoon dijon mustard
4 roasted garlic cloves (or use 2 fresh)
60 ml (2 fl oz/¼ cup) extra virgin olive oil
60 ml (2 fl oz/¼ cup) olive oil

1 large cauliflower, cut into florets
olive oil, for frying
lemon wedges, to serve

Potato and mushroom bake

serves 2–3

I first cooked this in a farmhouse near Sicily's Mount Etna, and just adore the simplicity of the approach.

Preheat the oven to 180°C (350°F/Gas 4). Spread the potato and onion slices in a flattish roasting tin. Dot the mushroom slices over the top and season with salt and freshly ground black pepper. Drizzle the olive oil generously over the top and bake for about 30 minutes, or until the potato is tender. Serve warm.

750 g (1 lb 10 oz) waxy potatoes, such as Dutch cream, thinly sliced
1 large red onion, thinly sliced
150 g (5½ oz) oyster mushrooms, sliced
1 large field mushroom, sliced
extra virgin olive oil, to drizzle

Cari the kelpie tears around in the frost, treating the frozen
 ground as a game, not a worry. The pigs are sturdy in the face of
a frozen trough, eager to traipse through mud when the day thaws.
 Priscilla's milk comes out warm and thick with cream, even on the
coldest morn. The smallholder isn't quite as resilient, but knows that
 the short winter days are punctuated with dishes that tend the soul.

Puddings and things
to eat while drinking tea

Not that you need an excuse to drink tea, but imagine a hot drop with an apple and sour cream slice, or macadamia and golden syrup butternut biscuits.

Winter means more gossiping around the tea cosy. More mugs of a steaming brew. In this chapter you'll find my suggestions for cake, for sweet snacks to make the tea last longer, for biscuits and slice and brownies.

And for days when the rib-sticking meals, the sturdy dishes and the substantial soups aren't enough, you're going to need pudding. What better than baked apples or a steamed pudding to make sure you don't end the meal hungry?

Recipes

Steamed cumquat marmalade pudding

serves 6–8

An old-fashioned steamed pudding is like childhood revisited.

Put the marmalade and golden syrup in a saucepan over low heat and stir until just softened and combined.

Using an electric beater, combine the butter and sugar until pale — it will stay crumbly because there's not a lot of butter. Beat in the egg until well combined, then fold in the flour and milk in two batches.

Grease a 1.25 litre (44 fl oz/5 cup) capacity pudding basin (mould) and lightly dust with a little flour. Pour the marmalade into the bottom of the basin, then tip in the pudding mixture and seal the lid. If you don't have a pudding basin use a heatproof bowl and cover the top with plastic wrap and then foil.

Tightly tie around the rim with kitchen string to seal, and make a handle from the string that you can use to help lift out the pudding later. Place the pudding bowl in a large saucepan and pour in enough hot water to come one-third of the way up the side of the basin. Bring to a simmer, then cover the pan and steam for about 2 hours, checking occasionally that there's enough water in the pan and topping up as needed.

Very gingerly remove the pudding tin from the water and take the cover off. You can either serve the pudding straight from the basin or invert onto a plate and serve warm with lightly whipped cream, perhaps scented with a pinch of ground cloves.

2 tablespoons cumquat marmalade or similar
1 tablespoon golden syrup or treacle
60 g (2¼ oz) butter, softened
200 g (7 oz) caster (superfine) sugar
1 egg
150 g (5½ oz/1 cup) self-raising flour, plus extra, for dusting
250 ml (9 fl oz/1 cup) milk

Caramel pear upside-down cake

serves 8

Pears are usually sold under-ripe (they ripen naturally at home) which is often ideal for cooking, even if you can't get the beurre bosc variety. If you aren't sure about making caramel, a more usual style of topping can be made using 185 g (6½ oz/1 cup) brown sugar dotted with the butter, and use poached or semi-cooked pears. The home-made caramel in this, however, does make for a better cake.

Grease a 22 cm (8½ inch) round cake tin and line the base and side with baking paper.

To make the caramel pears, put the sugar in a saucepan that is large enough to fit the pear halves in one layer. Cook over medium heat, without stirring, until it turns a light golden colour and starts to caramelise, then add the pears, cut side up. Cook for 10–15 minutes, shaking the pan occasionally, or until they soften — the juice from the pears will stop the caramel from burning. You want to balance the cooking of the pears (to a nice, tender softness) with the need to reduce the sugar to get a dark but not overly bitter caramel. Turn the pears over when they're soft on one side.

Remove the pears with a slotted spoon and arrange them, cut side down, in the base of the prepared tin. Scatter the walnuts in between the pears. Return the saucepan to the heat, increase the heat to high, and continue to cook the caramel in the pan. Add the butter and salt, stirring until well combined. Tip over the pears in the tin, then set aside to cool.

CARAMEL PEARS
150 g (5½ oz) sugar
3 large cooking pears, such as beurre bosc, peeled, halved and cored
50 g (1¾ oz/½ cup) walnuts or pecans
20 g (¾ oz) butter
a pinch of salt

CAKE
150 g (5½ oz/⅔ cup) caster (superfine) sugar
150 g (5½ oz) butter, softened
4 eggs
50 g (1¾ oz/½ cup) ground almonds
½ teaspoon ground cardamom
200 g (7 oz/1⅓ cups) self-raising flour
100 g (3½ oz) plain yoghurt

Preheat the oven to 180°C (350°F/Gas 4). To make the cake, put the sugar and butter in a bowl and use electric beaters to beat until light and creamy. Add the eggs, one at a time, beating well after each addition. This mix could look a bit curdled, which is absolutely normal so don't fret. Fold in the ground almonds and cardamom, then add half the flour, then the yoghurt, then the remaining flour, mixing well between ingredients.

Spoon the mixture over the pears in the tin, spreading it evenly (don't spread too vigorously or you'll move the pears and caramel). Bake on the middle shelf of the oven for 40–45 minutes, or until a skewer inserted into the centre of the cake comes out clean. Remove from the oven and allow to cool in the tin for 15 minutes. Invert onto a flat plate and remove the base, leaving the pear showing on top. Serve with a little pouring cream, if desired, and a nice cuppa.

Oh no. I couldn't possibly. I've already had one slice. A big slice with plenty of pear and dark caramel, which has soaked into the cake. No, thank you anyway. Well, if you're absolutely sure nobody else is going to eat it. Do you think I could have the recipe?

Kentish cherry and elderflower fruit pudding

serves 4

This is an old English way of making pudding using stale bread. It's a great winter pudding, but the best way I've tried it is with summer fruit, albeit preserved or frozen Kentish (small, sour) cherries. You can substitute them with morello cherries, apple, pear or cooked quince, and the elderflower with a few drops of orange blossom water, if you want to. I love the way it tastes a bit like bread and butter pudding, and a bit like egg custard. I don't, however, like to eat it very hot because it then tastes a bit too eggy. Make fresh breadcrumbs by pulsing crustless semi-stale bread in a food processor until very crumbly. Bought dry breadcrumbs simply won't work.

Preheat the oven to 180°C (350°F/Gas 4). Grease a 1.5 litre (52 fl oz/ 6 cup) capacity bar (loaf) tin or deep pie dish with a little butter and sprinkle lightly with a small amount of the sugar.

Lightly brown the almonds in a small frying pan over medium heat and when cool, grind them in a food processor until crumbled, but not quite as fine as ground almonds.

Put the eggs, salt and 55 g (2 oz/¼ cup) of the sugar in a bowl and beat until well combined, then stir in the milk. Add the breadcrumbs and set aside for 15 minutes to soak while you prepare the cherries.

Spread the cherries in the base of the pie dish and press down well. Mix the ground almonds, mandarin zest and elderflower cordial into the milk mixture, then pour this custard evenly over the cherries, pressing down a little to make it relatively flat. Sprinkle the remaining sugar over the top and bake for 20–30 minutes, or until the top is crusty. Serve warm or cold, but don't, if you have any self-respect, reheat in a microwave.

butter, for greasing
110 g (3¾ oz/½ cup) sugar
100 g (3½ oz/⅔ cup) blanched almonds
2 eggs
a generous pinch of salt
250 ml (9 fl oz/1 cup) milk
100 g (3½ oz/1¼ cups) fresh breadcrumbs
300 g (10½ oz) Kentish cherries, pitted (frozen are fine)
2 teaspoons finely grated mandarin zest, or other citrus zest
1 teaspoon elderflower cordial

Date, honey and ginger cake

serves 12

This is a lovely, rustic cake that makes the house smell like the home you wish you'd grown up in.

Preheat the oven to 180°C (350°F/Gas 4). Grease a 24 cm (9½ inch) square cake tin and line the base and sides with baking paper.

Put 250 ml (9 fl oz/1 cup) water in a saucepan and bring to the boil. Add the dates and ½ teaspoon of the bicarbonate of soda, then remove from the heat. Set aside.

Using electric beaters, whisk together the butter, sugar and honey in a bowl until light and fluffy. Add the eggs, one at a time, beating well after each addition. If it looks like it has curdled, it hasn't — everything will be just fine.

Fold in the flour, salt, remaining bicarbonate of soda, ginger, mixed spice, cinnamon and walnuts. Drain the dates, reserving the liquid, and fold the dates into the batter. Add enough water to the date liquid to make up 250 ml (9 fl oz/1 cup) in total, and stir this into the batter until well combined.

Pour the mixture into the tin and bake for about 60–70 minutes, or until a skewer inserted into the middle of the cake comes out clean. Remove from the oven and allow to cool in the tin for 20 minutes, then turn out and finish cooling on a wire rack. Store the cake in an airtight container for up to 5 days.

150 g (5½ oz/1 cup) roughly chopped pitted dates

1 teaspoon bicarbonate of soda (baking soda)

250 g (9 oz) butter, softened

250 g (9 oz) caster (superfine) sugar

350 g (12 oz/1 cup) honey

3 eggs

450 g (1 lb/3 cups) plain (all-purpose) flour

½ teaspoon salt

2 teaspoons ground ginger

2 teaspoons mixed (pumpkin pie) spice

1 teaspoon ground cinnamon

150 g (5½ oz/1½ cups) walnuts, lightly chopped

Brown sugar hazelnut biscuits

makes 16 biscuits

A friend's son made me some hazelnut biscuits so I tried re-creating them. Sorry James, these aren't yours, and they're not even close to the same, either. But they are just as good.

Preheat the oven to 160°C (315°F/Gas 2–3). Line two baking trays with baking paper.

Put the hazelnuts and almonds in a food processor and process until well broken up but not superfine — think crumbly, with some bits fine enough to classify as meal. Transfer to a small saucepan and add the sugar, butter and egg white. Place over low heat until the butter has just melted, then remove from the heat and allow to cool.

Take ½ tablespoon of the mixture at a time and roll into a ball. Repeat until all the mixture has been used. Roll each ball in the icing sugar to dust and arrange on the baking trays with enough room between each to allow for spreading. Bake in the oven for 15–20 minutes, or until the biscuits just start to change colour. Remove from the heat and allow to cool. Store the biscuits in an airtight container for up to 6 days.

75 g (2½ oz/½ cup) hazelnuts
75 g (2½ oz/½ cup) almonds
150 g (5½ oz/¾ cup) soft brown sugar
20 g (¾ oz) butter
1 egg white
2 tablespoons icing (confectioners') sugar, for dusting

Light, inconsequential, fragrant and with a little crunch of half-blended nut every now and then — that's the biscuit that you can eat any time of the day. And no, it wasn't me who stole one before breakfast.

Eccles cakes

makes 8

This fabulous currant pastry that originated near Manchester in the UK is simply heaven served with a good cuppa. If you make the full quantity of puff pastry you can freeze the leftover pastry for later use.

Preheat the oven to 230°C (450°F/Gas 8). Line a baking tray with baking paper.

Roll out the pastry to about 3 mm (⅛ inch) thick all over and use a 12 cm (4½ inch) round cookie cutter or similar to make eight rounds.

Put the butter in a saucepan over medium–low heat until melted, then add to the currants, citrus peel, nutmeg, allspice and sugar, stirring until the sugar dissolves. Put a large tablespoonful of the currant mixture in the centre of each pastry round, damp the edges of the pastry with a little of the egg glaze and draw them together to enclose the filling.

Place the pastries, crimped side down, on the prepared tray and press gently to create a nice pillow-shaped round. Score the top of the pastry gently with a sharp knife, (just the top, not all the way through), then brush with the egg glaze and sprinkle a little extra sugar over the top of each. Bake for 15–20 minutes, or until golden. Allow to cool before serving.

⅓ quantity puff pastry (see page 102–103)

30 g (1 oz) butter

120 g (4¼ oz/¾ cup) currants

1 tablespoon fresh citrus peel

a pinch of freshly grated nutmeg

a pinch of ground allspice

30 g (1 oz) caster (superfine) sugar, plus extra, for sprinkling

1 egg white, lightly beaten, to glaze

A very good, very chocolaty chocolate cake

serves 8

This cake, which is better the day after it's made, isn't pure chocolate like most of the recipes I've published over the years, but it is big on chocolate flavour and still a classic cake. It won me third place in the men's only chocolate cake section at the wonderfully rural Bream Creek Show in Tasmania. I was so excited I didn't stop bragging about it for a week.

Preheat the oven to 170°C (325°F/Gas 3). Grease an 18 cm (7 inch) spring-form cake tin and line it with baking paper.

Using electric beaters cream together the butter, sugar and vanilla in a large bowl. Add the eggs, one at a time, beating well after each addition — if the mixture looks a bit curdled, don't worry, it isn't; it'll come back together when the flour is added, if not before.

Beat in the chocolate, then the sour cream until just combined. Fold in the cocoa powder and flour and then add the ground almonds. Scrape into the prepared tin and smooth the top a bit. Bake for 40–50 minutes, or until a skewer inserted into the centre of the cake comes out clean. Remove from the oven and allow to cool in the tin for 10 minutes, before removing the outer ring and cooling on a wire rack.

To make the chocolate ganache icing, put the cream in a small saucepan and bring to the boil, remove from the heat and whisk in the chocolate. Return the pan to the heat if necessary to melt it, stirring until the mixture is smooth. Allow to set just enough so that it can be spread over the cake. Ice the cake from the centre outwards.

125 g (4½ oz) butter, softened

150 g (5½ oz/¾ cup) soft brown sugar

1 teaspoon natural vanilla extract

3 eggs

100 g (3½ oz) dark chocolate (about 50% cocoa is good), melted

100 g (3½ oz) sour cream

2 tablespoons unsweetened cocoa powder, sifted

100 g (3½ oz/⅔ cup) self-raising flour, sifted

125 g (4½ oz/1¼ cups) ground almonds

CHOCOLATE GANACHE ICING

100 ml (3½ fl oz) pouring (whipping) cream

250 g (9 oz/1⅔ cups) chopped dark chocolate (50% cocoa)

Bakewell tart

serves 8–10

Named after the English town of Bakewell where it originated, this tart usually has a layer of jam, but I've used dried fruit instead because it tastes good and it's got that slight wintry feel.

Put the dried fruit, mixed citrus peel and brandy in a bowl and mix to coat. Cover with plastic wrap and set aside for at least 5 hours, or overnight would be good.

Preheat the oven to 180°C (350°F/Gas 4). Grease a round 22 cm (8½ inch) fluted loose-based flan (tart) tin, about 3 cm (1¼ inches) deep.

To make the shortcrust pastry, sift the flour and icing sugar into a bowl and add the butter. Use your fingers to rub the butter through and break it into smaller pieces so the pieces of butter vary in size but are no bigger than a large pea. Add the egg yolk and lemon zest and lightly mix in using a knife. Sprinkle the chilled water in and lightly incorporate with the knife, then turn the pastry out onto a floured work surface and quickly knead until it comes together to form a ball. Wrap in plastic wrap and refrigerate for about 30 minutes.

Roll out the pastry on a lightly floured work surface or between two sheets of baking paper, until it is 2–3 mm (1/16–1/8 inch) thick all over and use it to line the prepared tin. Refrigerate for 30 minutes. Line the pastry with baking paper then fill it with baking beads, dried beans or rice. Blind bake for 10 minutes, or until the pastry is cooked on the edges. Remove the paper and weights and bake for a further 5 minutes to cook the base. Set aside until needed.

200 g (7 oz) mixed dried fruit, such as currants, sultanas (golden raisins) and chopped pitted dates
100 g (3½ oz) mixed citrus peel
60 ml (2 fl oz/¼ cup) brandy or sweet sherry
70 g (2½ oz) butter
110 g (3¾ oz/½ cup) caster (superfine) sugar
2 tablespoons ground almonds
2 eggs, separated

SHORTCRUST PASTRY
250 g (9 oz/1⅔ cups) plain (all-purpose) flour
80 g (2¾ oz) icing (confectioners') sugar
125 g (4½ oz) butter, chilled and cubed
2 egg yolks, lightly beaten
½ teaspoon finely grated lemon zest
1 tablespoon chilled water

continued...

Reduce the oven temperature to 160°C (315°F/Gas 2–3). To make the almond mixture, melt the butter in a small saucepan over medium heat, then add the sugar. Remove from the heat and transfer to a mixing bowl. Add the ground almonds and use electric beaters to aerate the mixture — this will take about 1–2 minutes. When cool, beat in the egg yolks, one at a time, until well combined.

In a separate bowl, whisk the egg whites until soft peaks form. Fold gently into the almond mixture. Spread the fruit evenly over the base of the pastry case, then carefully pour in the almond mixture. Bake for 30–35 minutes, or until cooked. Allow to cool in the oven — the top will sink a little and that's fine. Serve at room temperature.

Chocolate, banana and honey pie

serves 6

Wouldn't it be good to live off starters and pud? Main courses, methinks, are weekday fodder — something you cook when you have only the minutes and the vigour for cooking one dish. With entrées we get more variety, more flavours and less of just one ingredient. Dessert is all sweetness, brightness and light. The main course, though, tends to be too much of too little. And if you're like me and eat dessert first on occasion, it's also too late.

Preheat the oven to 180°C (350°F/Gas 4). Grease a 22 cm (8½ inch) round pie dish or flan (tart) tin, about 3 cm (1¼ inches) deep.

Roll out the pastry on a lightly floured work surface to about 5 mm (¼ inch) thick all over and use it to line the pie dish. Refrigerate for about 20–30 minutes. Line the pastry with baking paper then fill it with baking beads, dried beans or rice. Blind bake for 10–15 minutes, or until the pastry is cooked on the edges. Remove the paper and weights and bake for a further 5 minutes to cook the base.

While the pastry cools, peel the bananas and cut into 5 mm (¼ inch) thick slices on a sharp angle. Once the pastry has cooled, lay the slices over the pie base in a couple of layers, covering any gaps in the bottom layer with the second layer. Mix the honey, vanilla and sour cream together until smooth, then fold in the chocolate and coffee quickly so that the chocolate doesn't set in the cream. Immediately spread the chocolate mixture over the banana. Refrigerate for at least 2–3 hours so that the chocolate mixture can set. Serve with rum ice cream or just rum.

1 quantity shortcrust pastry (see page 194)

2 bananas

70 g (2½ oz) honey, warmed slightly if too thick

1 teaspoon natural vanilla extract

300 g (10½ oz) sour cream

200 g (7 oz/1⅓ cups) chopped dark chocolate (50% cocoa), melted

1½ tablespoons espresso coffee, or very strong instant or plunger coffee

Apple and sour cream slice

makes 36 pieces

This moist-topped slice is best eaten the same day it's made, or soon after.

Preheat the oven to 160°C (315°F/Gas 2–3). Grease a 25 cm (10 inch) square cake tin and line the base and sides with baking paper.

Put the flour, sugar and coconut in a mixing bowl and stir to combine. Add the butter and vanilla and mix well until evenly combined. Press firmly into the base of the prepared tin and bake for 20 minutes.

Remove the slice base from the oven and increase the oven temperature to 180°C (350°F/Gas 4). Put the eggs and sour cream in a bowl and stir until smooth. Spread the apple evenly over the base (you don't need the juice that falls out of it), sprinkle the sugar over the top and pour the sour cream mixture over, spreading evenly. Bake the slice in the oven for 20–30 minutes, or until the top is set and starting to colour. Remove from the oven and allow to cool completely before slicing with a sharp knife into 3–4 cm (1¼–1½ inch) squares. Store in an airtight container for up to 4 days.

200 g (7 oz/1⅓ cups) self-raising flour

150 g (5½ oz/⅔ cup) caster (superfine) sugar

90 g (3¼ oz/1 cup) desiccated coconut

125 g (4½ oz) butter, melted

1 teaspoon natural vanilla extract

2 eggs, lightly beaten

300 g (10½ oz) sour cream

2 apples, peeled and coarsely grated by hand

2 tablespoons soft brown sugar

Skimming stones over the river, muddy puddles and bloodied knees. Licking spatulas and baking and eating slices. The only difference between being an adult and a kid is that when you're all grown up you can be trusted to take hot things from the oven.

Exceptionally good brownies

makes about 25

I like my brownies a bit rich and chocolaty, especially when they're home-made. If you only have chocolate with a low cocoa content, add 1–2 tablespoons unsweetened cocoa powder to bulk up that gorgeous chocolate flavour.

Preheat the oven to 180°C (350°F/Gas 4). Grease a 20 x 30 cm (8 x 12 inch) baking tin or similar and line the base and sides with baking paper — the bigger the tray, the less cakey the end result.

Put the butter and chocolate in a heatproof bowl and place over a saucepan of barely simmering water, making sure the base of the bowl does not touch the water, and stir until melted. Set aside to cool to just above room temperature.

Using electric beaters, beat together the eggs, sugar and salt in a large bowl until pale. Fold in the cooled chocolate mixture, followed by the flour and last of all, fold in the walnuts; try not to overmix or it'll lose some of its air. Spoon into the prepared tin and bake for 25–35 minutes; when tested with a skewer it won't come out completely clean like it does when testing a cake, but it shouldn't have raw mix on it either.

Remove from the oven and allow to cool in the tin, then turn out and cut into squares to serve. Store in an airtight container for 3–4 days at the most.

150 g (5½ oz) butter
200 g (7 oz/1⅓ cups) chopped dark chocolate (about 70% cocoa)
4 eggs
300 g (10½ oz/1⅓ cups) sugar
a pinch of salt
100 g (3½ oz/⅔ cup) plain (all-purpose) flour
150 g (5½ oz/1½ cups) walnuts, broken up a bit

Slice

makes 54 pieces

We call this Sloice, in the same way that we say it's roolly, roolly noice. Not Coconut Sloice, or Sultana Sloice. Just Sloice. It comes from one of those recipe cards so many of us have handwritten and keep in a box, courtesy of the late Betty Sugars. Here I've included a cooking temperature, the size of the baking tin and a few more details than written on the original recipe card. Entitled, simply, Slice, one word says all you need to know about the sweet you have to have when friends drop by for a cup of tea.

Preheat the oven to 180°C (350°F/Gas 4). Grease a 28 x 18 cm (11¼ x 7 inch) baking tin and line the base and sides with baking paper.

Put the butter and golden syrup in a small saucepan over low heat and stir until just melted. Set aside.

Put the coconut, sugar, flour and sultanas in a large mixing bowl and stir to combine. Add the butter mixture and the egg and stir until well combined. Pour into the prepared tin and bake in the middle of the oven for 20–30 minutes, or until golden — the slice may sink a bit after cooking and that's okay. Allow to cool in the tin, then cut into 3 cm (1¼ inch) squares or similar and serve early and often. The slice can be stored in an airtight container for 3–4 days.

125 g (4½ oz) butter
1 tablespoon golden syrup
90 g (3¼ oz/1 cup) desiccated coconut
165 g (5¾ oz/¾ cup) caster (superfine) sugar
150 g (5½ oz/1 cup) self-raising flour
125 g (4½ oz) sultanas (golden raisins)
1 egg, lightly beaten

Peanut and chocolate chip biscuits

makes about 40

If you use a 100 per cent pure peanut paste for this (from a health food shop or similar) it won't have quite the right amount of fat or sugar because most peanut butter has oil and sugar added. If you do use a pure peanut paste, add another 30 g (1 oz) butter and 30 g (1 oz) dark brown sugar to make up for it.

Preheat the oven to 180°C (350°F/Gas 4). Line two baking trays with baking paper.

Using electric beaters, combine the sugar and butter together in a bowl until just smooth, then beat in the egg and vanilla. Beat in the peanut butter, then fold in the salt, bicarbonate of soda and flour. Mix until just combined, then fold in the chocolate chips.

Take 1 tablespoonful of the mixture at a time and roll into balls. Lay on a tray in rows, and press each ball down with a fork to about 1 cm (½ inch) thick (the chocolate chips can make them a bit tricky to press down). Bake in the centre of the oven for about 10 minutes, or until nicely tanned, but not going dark. Remove from the oven and allow to cool on a wire rack. Store in an airtight container and serve often with a wickedly hot cup of tea. These biscuits will keep well in the container for about 3–4 days.

150 g (5½ oz/¾ cup) dark brown sugar

100 g (3½ oz) butter, softened

1 egg

½ teaspoon natural vanilla extract

300 g (10½ oz) crunchy peanut butter

½ teaspoon salt

½ teaspoon bicarbonate of soda (baking soda)

225 g (8 oz/1½ cups) plain (all-purpose) flour

200 g (7 oz/1¼ cups) dark chocolate chips

Baked apples with dates and brown sugar

serves 4

Come on, baked apples may not be fashionable but you know you want them. You can also add some nuts to the filling if you have some floating around. Pistachios would be nice.

To make the cinnamon cream, whisk all of the ingredients together in a small bowl until it is a soft, moussey consistency. Cover with plastic wrap and refrigerate until needed.

Preheat the oven to 180°C (350°F/Gas 4). Core the apples all the way through using a corer if you have one, or a small knife if you don't. If you don't want the skin to blow apart, cut a fine line through the skin from one end of the apple to the other. Seed and chop the dates into smallish bits and mix with the currants and lemon zest. Pack the date mixture into the centre of each apple and press some brown sugar into the top of each one, then crown this stuffing with a knob of butter.

Put 125 ml (4 fl oz/½ cup) water into the base of a baking tin, then put the apples in and bake for 40–45 minutes, or until very soft. They can take longer or less, depending on what variety of apples you have, how fresh they are and just what the real temperature of your oven is. Serve with the cinnamon cream and try to scrape out some of those yummy pan juices, too.

CINNAMON CREAM
150 ml (5 fl oz) pouring (whipping) cream
1–2 tablespoons icing (confectioners') sugar
a pinch of ground cinnamon, or to taste
a small pinch of ground cloves

4 cooking apples, such as granny smith
4 fresh dates
1 tablespoon currants
1 teaspoon finely grated lemon zest
2 tablespoons soft brown sugar
20 g (¾ oz) butter

Individual golden syrup and hazelnut puddings

serves 6

This is a variation on a maple syrup pudding I make, though with more nuts and more of that wonderful golden syrup flavour.

Preheat the oven to 200°C (400°F/Gas 6). Grease six 300 ml (10½ fl oz) dariole moulds or big cups with a vague smear of butter.

Put the hazelnuts in a food processor and process until crumbly but not too fine. Set aside.

Using electric beaters, combine the butter and sugar until pale and fluffy. Add the eggs, one at a time, beating well after each addition. Fold in the lemon zest and flour first, then the hazelnuts. Spoon this mixture evenly into the six moulds and then spoon the golden syrup over the top.

Cover each mould with foil and place in a roasting tin. Pour enough boiling water into the tin so it comes 2 cm (¾ inch) up the sides of the moulds and bake for 30 minutes. Remove the foil, lower the oven temperature to 180°C (350°F/Gas 4) and continue baking for about 15 minutes, or until a skewer inserted into the centre of the puddings comes out clean and the puddings are a deep golden colour. Serve warm in their cooking dishes with ice cream.

100 g (3½ oz/⅔ cup) hazelnuts

200 g (7 oz) butter, softened, plus extra, for greasing

150 g (5½ oz/¾ cup) soft brown sugar

3 eggs

finely grated zest of 1 lemon

150 g (5½ oz/1 cup) self-raising flour, sifted

175 g (6 oz/½ cup) golden syrup

Warm. Sweet. A place to dunk the spoon and rejoice in the fact that nights are long and summer far away. Pudding — the only friend you need when the mist is sinking into the valley and the fire is going. Though a real friend to share it with would probably make the season even sweeter.

Jam tart

serves 8

In Italy they call this a crostata. But unlike many of their dishes, it does have a nice easy translation that's equally appetising in English; it's just a jam tart that's free-form in shape. A food processor on pulse setting makes the pastry faster and easier to prepare.

Put 150 g (5½ oz/1 cup) of the flour in a mixing bowl with the baking powder, sugar and 1 pinch of the salt. Add the vanilla and egg and work into a dough using your fingertips. Work in the butter, only until it comes together (not evenly spread) then add the remaining flour. Mix just long enough to get the dough to hold together, cover with plastic wrap, then refrigerate for 30 minutes.

Preheat the oven to 200°C (400°F/Gas 6). Flour a piece of baking paper and roll the pastry out on it into a rough circle with a 35 cm (14 inch) diameter — it can overhang because you're going to fold in the edges. Lift the baking paper with the pastry and transfer to a baking tray. Smear the jam in a rough circle on the pastry leaving a 6 cm (2½ inch) border around the edges. Fold an edge of the pastry towards the centre to cover the jam, making a crust of about 4 cm (1½ inches), then work your way around the tart, folding the edges over to create folds in the pastry as you go. Each one will look different and that's exactly what you want.

Whisk the extra egg and sugar together with the remaining salt and use to brush the exposed ring of pastry, making sure you cover all of the folds, but being careful not to let the egg run onto the jam. Bake towards the top of the oven for 30–40 minutes, or until the pastry is golden coloured and cooked.

300 g (10½ oz/2 cups) plain (all-purpose) flour, sifted
½ teaspoon baking powder
100 g (3½ oz) caster (superfine) sugar, plus 1 teaspoon extra
2 pinches of salt
½ teaspoon natural vanilla extract
1 egg, lightly beaten, plus 1 egg extra
120 g (4¼ oz) butter, chilled and cubed
150 g (5½ oz) plum or berry jam

Macadamia and golden syrup butternut biscuits

makes about 18

These delectable biscuits are the most perfect way to eat golden syrup and nuts at the same time. If you don't have macadamias one day, you can substitute with almonds, though they won't be quite as yummy that way.

Preheat the oven to 170°C (325°F/Gas 3). Line two baking trays with baking paper.

Put the sugar, golden syrup and butter in a small saucepan over low heat and stir just until the butter and golden syrup are melted. Allow to cool enough so you can touch the mixture. This is really important because if the mixture is too hot it will cook the flour and your biscuits will end up a very different texture.

Put the macadamia nuts, flour, oats and salt in a mixing bowl. Stir in the golden syrup mixture, being sure to scrape out all the syrup from the saucepan. Stir to mix well.

Take 1 tablespoonful of the mixture at a time and roll into a ball. Repeat with the remaining mixture. Press them onto the prepared trays, leaving some room for them to spread a little. Bake for 12–17 minutes, or until a golden colour — it pays to turn the trays around after 10 minutes. Remove from the oven, allow to cool for 5 minutes, then transfer to wire racks to cool completely. These biscuits can be stored in an airtight container for 3–4 days.

100 g (3½ oz) caster (superfine) sugar
70 g (2½ oz) golden syrup
100 g (3½ oz) butter
100 g (3½ oz) macadamia nuts, coarsely crushed
100 g (3½ oz/⅔ cup) self-raising flour
100 g (3½ oz/1 cup) rolled (porridge) oats
a pinch of salt

Spazzacamino
(ice cream with ground coffee and whisky)

Spazzacamino, *chimney sweep's ice cream from Italy, is so-called because the coffee looks like ash from the chimney and the smoky whisky smells like a fire. It's a grown-up dessert that needs a quality creamy ice cream to really shine.*

All you'll need is a large scoop of vanilla ice cream per serve, sprinkle over 1 teaspoon of finely ground coffee beans, then add 1–2 tablespoons of single malt whisky, to taste.

To the man who talks to me in the street as he sweeps his driveway. To the clothes shop assistant who understands I've gone in to be helped, not humiliated. To the real estate agent who realises he is dealing with people at one of the most vulnerable times in their lives (there must be one out there). To the warmth of humanity when you least expect it — this one's for you.

Chelsea buns with dates, treacle and walnuts

makes 8 scrolls

I've used treacle for a more adult, slightly bitter flavour in these, but if it's for the kids, you're better off using golden syrup. Some might call these cinnamon scrolls. Everybody will like the sticky end result.

To make the dough, put the flour, yeast and salt in a mixing bowl and stir well to combine; make a well in the centre. Mix the honey and milk in a separate bowl. Pour the milk mixture, egg and butter into the dry ingredients and use a knife to stir in a circular fashion, incorporating the flour from the edges on each turn. When it gets thick, start to knead by hand. If you have an electric mixer with a dough hook, use that. Knead for about 6–8 minutes, to make a smooth and elastic dough. Brush a large clean bowl with a little oil and roll the dough around in it to coat in a fine film of oil. Cover the bowl with plastic wrap and set aside for about 1 hour, or until the dough has doubled in size. Don't be fussy about it, just make sure it's risen.

Preheat the oven to 180°C (350°F/Gas 4). Lightly grease a baking tray. Knead the dough again just enough to incorporate all the oil. Roll it out on a lightly floured work surface using a rolling pin (and your hands to push and stretch) to make a 20 x 30 cm (8 x 12 inch) rectangle, about 1 cm (½ inch) thick (or slightly less).

To make the topping, mash the sugar and cinnamon into the softened butter. Spread this evenly over the dough, then drizzle half the treacle over the top. Scatter the dates and walnuts evenly over. Roll the dough up along the short side into a long log. Cut this log into 8 evenly sized slabs, and stand them upright on the tray, close enough to hold each other up, though they should expand a bit as they cook. Drizzle the remaining treacle over the tops and bake for 30–40 minutes, or until golden. Remove from the oven and allow to cool a little. Pull apart and serve to people with clean fingers so they can lick all the yummy goo off their hands.

DOUGH

330 g (11¾ oz) plain (all-purpose) flour
2 teaspoons dried yeast
1 teaspoon salt
½ teaspoon honey or sugar
170 ml (5½ fl oz/⅔ cup) tepid milk (body temperature)
1 egg, lightly beaten
50 g (1¾ oz) butter, melted
vegetable oil, for greasing

TOPPING

100 g (3½ oz) caster (superfine) sugar
2 teaspoons ground cinnamon
80 g (2¾ oz) butter, softened
150 g (5½ oz) treacle or golden syrup
70 g (2½ oz) pitted dates, finely chopped
70 g (2½ oz) walnuts, crushed

Hot drinks and a nibble

So, you're still thirsty are you? Sick of tea and don't want to drink that rain water because it comes ice-cold from the tap and that isn't exactly what you want in winter? How about a warm barley water, scented with mandarins because they're in the shops right now? What about blood orange, with hot tonic and gin? Or how about a salty snack of celery heart with anchovy sauce, a mountain of light-as-air cheese puffs, or a ham hock and white bean terrine?

You know you want something different to celebrate the season. Well, there's always a lightly spiced hot chocolate to send you into a state of bliss.

Recipes

Classic whisky hot toddy

serves 1

Put 200 ml (7 fl oz) water in a saucepan over high heat and bring to the boil. Reduce the heat to low, add the lemon juice and honey, stirring well until the honey is dissolved. Remove from the heat, add the whisky, to taste, and pour into a warmed glass or mug. Perhaps add a half slice of lemon, too, to give a hint of bitterness.

2 teaspoons freshly squeezed lemon juice
1–2 teaspoons honey
2 tablespoons whisky
1 lemon slice (optional)

A hot toddy is a warm drink with alcohol in it. Most think no further than the classic (and fantastic) lemon, whisky and honey variety famed for its curative, restorative power when you have a cold. (The honey soothes the throat, the lemon has vitamin C and the whisky helps you sleep, or so the legend goes.) But any warm alcoholic drink is a hot toddy. And most are pretty good.

Cheese puffs

makes about 60

Inconsequential little balls of cheesy air, also known as gougères, make perfect finger food. These savoury choux pastries can be made a day ahead and stored in an airtight container. They also freeze well.

Preheat the oven to 180°C (350°F/Gas 4). Line two baking trays with baking paper.

Put the butter, salt and 250 ml (9 fl oz/1 cup) water in a saucepan over medium heat and simmer until the butter just melts. Add the flour all at once and beat continuously with a wooden spoon until the mixture is glossy and comes away from the side of the pan. Remove from the heat and beat in the eggs, one at a time, waiting until the dough comes back to a nice uniform consistency between each egg. Add the grated cheese, season with freshly ground black pepper, and beat to combine.

Put teaspoon-sized blobs (or pipe little balls) onto the baking trays in neat rows, leaving room for them to expand. Top each one with a little finely grated cheese. Bake for about 25 minutes, or until puffed and cooked through. Cool on wire racks and serve at room temperature.

125 g (4½ oz) butter
½ teaspoon salt
200 g (7 oz/1⅓ cups) plain (all-purpose) flour
5 eggs
100 g (3½ oz/1 cup) grated gruyére cheese, plus 50 g (1¾ oz) extra, finely grated

Blood orange and gin hot toddy

serves 1–2

The blood orange season is winter, and while a glass of the fresh juice is already hard to pass up, with a touch of gin and warmed, it's unbeatable.

Put the tonic water in a saucepan over high heat and bring to the boil. Add the blood orange juice and heat until nearly boiling again, then remove from the heat and add the gin, to taste. Pour into a warmed glass or mug and serve immediately.

250 ml (9 fl oz/1 cup) tonic water
100 ml (3½ fl oz) freshly squeezed blood orange juice
1–2 tablespoons gin

Warm spiced apple juice

serves 4

A woman next to my stall at the local growers' market sells hot apple juice to the crowds to keep them warm. I'm in love with the idea and the taste, though I do like it more with a bit of brandy or calvados (apple brandy) added at the end.

Put the apple juice and water in a saucepan over high heat and bring to the boil. Add the lemon slice, cinnamon and cloves, reduce the heat to low and simmer for about 10 minutes, or until it is spiced to your liking. If you're really up for a winter warmer, slip a little brandy or calvados into the glasses when you go to serve it.

500 ml (17 fl oz/2 cups) good-quality cloudy apple juice
500 ml (17 fl oz/2 cups) boiling water
1 lemon slice
1 cinnamon stick
8 whole cloves
brandy or calvados (optional), to taste

Mulled wine with seville orange and cardamom

serves 4

Sensational, bitter seville oranges have a very short season and a limited use compared to oranges that are eaten fresh as fruit. That's why it's best to make use of them in something wonderful, like this gently warmed wine. Unlike most recipes that use wine, I don't recommend a very good drop, but something that's pleasant enough to drink.

Put 250 ml (9 fl oz/1 cup) of the wine in a saucepan with the remaining ingredients over high heat. Bring nearly to the boil, then reduce the heat to low and simmer for about 15 minutes — this will extract the flavours from the spices and orange without altering the wine too much. If you boil the wine the alcohol will dissipate, which is fine, but I like to keep some alcohol in, so that's why I add most of the wine later.

Add the remaining wine and heat until it's steaming but not boiling. Taste for sweetness, adding extra sugar if desired, then pour into warmed glasses and serve immediately.

1 litre (35 fl oz/4 cups) red wine
1 cinnamon stick
4 seville orange slices
10 green cardamom pods
50 g (1¾ oz/¼ cup) soft brown sugar, plus extra, to taste

Ham hock and white bean terrine

serves 10

This recipe comes from my mate Ross who I run a market stall with. I wasn't that excited by the idea at first — until I tasted it. There's this marvellous effect of rich meat against the mealiness of the beans.

Put the hocks into a large saucepan with the onion, bay leaves, juniper berries and enough water to just cover them. Bring to the boil over high heat, then reduce the heat to low and simmer for about 2 hours, or until the meat is tender. Remove the hocks (reserving the cooking liquid in the pan; discard the bay leaves and juniper berries). When cool enough to handle, pull the meat from the bones and shred into bite-sized pieces, discarding the bones and fat.

Put the beans into the ham hock cooking liquid and bring to the boil. Reduce the heat and simmer for about 1½ hours, or until the beans are tender. The time can vary a lot, depending on how old the beans are, how well soaked they are and the temperature in your kitchen on the night you soaked them. Test them regularly after about 45 minutes to be sure — you want them tender, but not falling apart. Drain well and cool.

Preheat the oven to 170°C (325°F/Gas 3) and line a 1.5 litre (52 fl oz/6 cup) capacity terrine tin or similar with plastic wrap, allowing for a good overhang on all sides.

In a large bowl, mix together the beans with the ham, pork, nutmeg and salt. Spoon the bean mixture into the tin, pressing firmly to remove any air pockets. Fold the plastic wrap over the top, then cover the top with foil. Place in a large roasting tin and pour enough hot water into the tin to come 3 cm (1¼ inches) up the sides of the terrine tin. Bake for about 45 minutes — it will have shrunk a bit from the sides of the tin and a skewer inserted into the middle should come out hot. Allow to cool in the tin, then refrigerate after about 30 minutes to cool completely.

When ready to serve, strip away the foil and plastic and scrape away any fat from the sides of the terrine. Cut into 1.5 cm (⅝ inch) slices and serve as an entrée, or as a snack with drinks, with some sliced pickled onions and a salad of winter greens.

2 x 500 g (1 lb 2 oz) smoked ham hocks
1 onion
2 bay leaves
5 juniper berries
200 g (7 oz/1 cup) dried haricot beans or other white beans, soaked overnight, rinsed and drained
300 g (10½ oz) minced (ground) pork
¼ whole nutmeg, ground (about ¼ teaspoon)
a generous pinch of salt

Hot mandarin barley water

serves 4

This is a warm take on the summer classic, lemon barley water, given the gorgeous fragrant oils from the skin of a mandarin. If you don't have sugar cubes, you can tip the boiling water over the skins of the citrus to try to extract the flavour, but cubes do a better job at harnessing the oils. You can simmer the skins in the barley water to get a little more adult bitterness in the drink, too. If there's ever a time to use organic fruit, then this might be it, so you can be sure there's no pesticide or herbicide residue on the skin. You can use the leftover barley in a braise or soup.

Put the barley and 1 litre (35 fl oz/4 cups) water in a saucepan over high heat and bring to the boil. Reduce the heat to low and simmer for about 20 minutes, or until the liquid looks cloudy.

Meanwhile, rub the sugar cubes over the mandarin and lemon skins, using each side as a scourer to extract the oils (the clue to success will be the colour change in the sugar). Add the cubes to the pan as you go. I tend to find that some sugar cubes dissolve as you rub, so dip the fruit in the water at the end to rinse off any oil and sugar still on the skin. Juice the mandarin and lemon and add the juices to the barley water. Stir well and strain.

Reheat the barley water, if necessary, and serve warm on a cold day. If using the brandy, add it to taste after the barley water has been poured into hot glasses.

100 g (3½ oz) pearl barley, rinsed and drained
8 sugar cubes
1 mandarin, scrubbed and dried
1 lemon, scrubbed and dried
brandy (optional), to taste

Spiced hot chocolate

serves 4

Have you ever noticed the texture of hot chocolate in some of the best cafes? It's a bit thicker than normal milk. The secret is in using a light starch to help the chocolate linger longer in the mouth — which means more sensation of chocolate without more chocolate. You don't have to use the starch, just add a splash of cream if you like a richer mouthfeel.

Put the milk, cinnamon, star anise and vanilla in a saucepan over high heat and bring nearly to the boil. Turn off the heat and let it stand for 15 minutes, with a lid on, to prevent a skin forming. Strain and reheat in a clean saucepan. Add the chocolate to the pan as the milk comes to a simmer and whisk until it has dissolved.

Whisk the cocoa and rice flour with a splash of water or more milk in a bowl, then add 2 tablespoons of the hot milk and whisk to combine. Whisk the cocoa mixture into the hot milk in the pan, return to the heat and bring nearly to the boil, stirring constantly. Add sugar, to taste, and serve hot.

800 ml (28 fl oz) milk
1 small cinnamon stick
1 whole star anise
1 vanilla bean, split lengthways
150 g (5½ oz/1 cup) chopped good-quality dark chocolate (70% cocoa)
2 tablespoons unsweetened cocoa powder
1 teaspoon rice or potato flour (optional)
1 tablespoon sugar

Celery heart with anchoiade

serves 8

Anchoiade, as the name suggests, is an anchovy paste, which tastes better with good-quality anchovies. I use an egg yolk to cut down the strength of the paste. This dish is much better if made a day ahead to let the pungency of the garlic mellow and the flavours blend.

Crush the garlic and anchovies to a fine paste using a mortar and pestle, or use a mini food processor. Add the egg yolk and mix to combine, then gradually add the olive oil in a thin stream, stirring continuously, until well combined and smooth.

Refrigerate the paste overnight, if possible, to let it mature, then serve the next day with the celery.

5 garlic cloves
8 anchovy fillets
1 egg yolk
200 ml (7 fl oz) extra virgin olive oil
pale hearts from 2 bunches of celery, rinsed

Index

Acknowledgments

Thank you, my lovely Sadie, for letting me trash the kitchen and fill our farmhouse with a crew of people. Again. And for allowing me the gift of fatherhood.

Thanks to Terry O'Neil for letting us traipse around his farm and steal some of his produce, and Marcus Hamilton for his artichokes. I raise a glass (of hot toddy) to Ann Dechaineux, LJ Struthers of The Maker and Jenene Oates for padding out my array of old and new cooking equipment and serving dishes for the shots, and Al Campbell for helping out on the last day with cooking, cleaning and packing all those same props.

Sincere gratitude to the sensationally talented Charlotte Bell who styled about a quarter of the book; we wish she'd been on board from the start. To the irrepressible Michelle Crawford who cooked like an angel and took my ideas and ran with them, I give thanks.

Thanks to far-flung editors Jo Glynn and Jacqueline Blanchard for finding my mistakes and fixing them. And to Juliet Rogers and Kylie Walker and the team at Murdoch Books for once more allowing my ideas to gain air.

I'm indebted to Ross O'Meara, a mate who turned his hand to my recipes with aplomb (and let me steal a couple of his).

And of course I have to salute my dear friend and photographer Alan Benson. He came and stayed on the farm while the book was still just a dream, with many recipes yet to be written, and captured the season and shot and helped style the food. Without your wit, wisdom and occasional whinge, AB, a stunning book like this simply wouldn't be possible.

Published in 2011 by Murdoch Books Pty Limited

Murdoch Books Australia
Pier 8/9
23 Hickson Road
Millers Point NSW 2000
Phone: +61 (0) 2 8220 2000
Fax: +61 (0) 2 8220 2558
www.murdochbooks.com.au

Murdoch Books UK Limited
Erico House, 6th Floor
93–99 Upper Richmond Road
Putney, London SW15 2TG
Phone: +44 (0) 20 8785 5995
Fax: +44 (0) 20 8785 5985
www.murdochbooks.uk.co

Publisher: Kylie Walker
Photographer: Alan Benson
Stylist: Charlotte Bell

Editor: Jacqueline Blanchard
Designer: Tania Gomes

CFO: Jonathan Koop

National Library of Australia Cataloguing-in-Publication Data:

Author: Evans, Matthew, 1966–
Title: Winter on the Farm / Matthew Evans.
ISBN: 978-1-74266-227-5 (hbk.)
Notes: Includes index.
Subjects: Cooking.
Dewey Number: 641.5

A catalogue record for this book is available from the British Library.

Printed by 1010 Printing International Limited, China.

IMPORTANT: Those who might be at risk from the effects of salmonella poisoning (the
elderly, pregnant women, young children and those suffering from immune deficiency
diseases) should consult their doctor with any concerns about eating raw eggs.

OVEN GUIDE: You may find cooking times vary depending on the oven you are using.
For fan-forced ovens, as a general rule, set the oven temperature to 20°C (35°F) lower
than indicated in the recipe.